Dear Passenger:

Welcome to My Wacky World as a Flight Attendant

Dear Passenger:

Welcome to My Wacky World as a Flight Attendant

by

Elizabeth Calwell

REALIZATION
ℬ PRESS ℭ

ISBN: 978-1-944662-25-7

Cover Design and Illustration by Irfan Budhiharjo © 2018

Dedication

I want to thank my husband for his loving support and patience.

SOUTHERN LINGO and other polite alternatives to: "What the hell are you thinking?"

Bless your heart!

Puhleeeze!

REeeaLLY!

Well, isn't that nice?

Table of Contents

TAXI OUT

AFTER TAKEOFF

PREFACE

COME ALONG WITH ME

Dear Passenger,

Hello! Nice to meet you. Why don't you come have a seat beside me? Yes, I mean you. We both know the jump seat is authorized only for crew members, but this one time we'll make an exception so you can get the feel of what it's like to walk in my shoes. When all the flight attendants disappear for takeoff and landing they're taking a designated jump seat closest to all door exits. On this flight, I'm in coach. So you can join me on the most uncomfortable seat in the house, in the aft (back) galley of the plane. There's not much room on this double jump seat, which folds down out of the wall like a built-in ironing board. Come on…have a seat. You can buckle up for this trip right beside me. We've finished our beverage service, so now I have time to talk.

You know there's something magical about sitting on this cramped-hard jump seat that makes perfect strangers tell each other intimate secrets. Or is it being in the galley? We don't call it "galley gossip" for nothing.

DING! Shoot, that's a call light! Excuse me, but I have to go see what that passenger wants.

The man seated in 26A asked, "Oh miss, where's my remote control for that television?" He pointed to the overhead monitors for the entire airplane.

I winked at his wife, and said, "On this airplane we only give the remote control to the wives."

I thought he was going to have a heart attack but his wife pursed her mouth in a smirk of approval.

She gave him a condescending glance and said, "Wow that was a blow to your recliner mentality."

I left him sniveling and mumbling about the remote. Bless his heart!

Let me tell you, people are very curious about my occupation. You wouldn't believe how many times I'm asked where I've been that day, where I'm going, how long my trip will be and how many days a week or month I work.

I'm, of course, referring to the casual traveler, not the business customer who flies almost as much as I do. Frequent flyers know about the major hassles required nowadays just to get through the airport. They know not to try to get sympathy from a flight attendant about what time they got up that morning or how many days they're away from home.

Leisure passengers, when they finally board the airplane, are excited to be going on their vacations to exotic locations. In the back of their minds they think that working this job is like that, too. They expect all the crew members on the plane to share that same exuberance, or maybe that was back in the good old days when flying was glamorous. Film enhanced that romantic image, like the TV show Pan Am and Leo DiCaprio's movie Catch Me if You Can.

Could this be where the attraction to my occupation comes from?

"The fascination with airplanes and anything associated with them starts early."

My neighbor, Debbie said this to me out in my front yard as an airplane flew overhead in the clouds. Her little grandson shrieked with excitement as he pointed up to the sky. I understood, because when I was little I couldn't comprehend how a jet could get off the ground either. *I still don't.*

DING! Excuse me again. I need to answer that call light.

I'm back and I can tell you, as soon as I walked up to those two ladies, I could see they were having an elbow-fight over the armrest between them. I asked one of the women if she needed anything.

"She called me stupid." She pointed her finger at the lady beside her.

"Well, she called me fat." The other lady pointed back.

Speaking through clenched teeth, they both jockeyed for possession of the armrest. I never taught kindergarten, so I wasn't quite sure how to handle this situation. I looked around for any empty seat to separate these two, but the flight was completely full. I pulled out two magazines from the seat-back pocket. I propped up one magazine on one side of the armrest so it blocked that side from being used by one of them. Then I did the same on the other side with the other magazine.

I told one lady, "Don't cross over this magazine."

Then I turned to the other lady and said, "And don't you cross over the magazine from your side either."

Now that neither one of them had access to the armrest, they both glared at me. "And don't talk to each other either."

One lady nearby, one of many who had to listen to this brawl, caught my eye and mouthed, "Thank you."

I found out both of those women had husbands and children on the flight. But do you think those husbands said anything to help me out? Not a word. I guess they knew better than to throw fuel on the fire.

Now where was I? Oh yes, my job. Most people want to know how flight attendants choose where to fly. It works like this: we bid or request a trip schedule for the following month. The seniority-based assignment comes from a list put together by the airline. Each bid includes the number of days on duty, days off, and trip destinations. Bids also designate the flight attendant's assigned position on the plane.

We submit our bid selections by computer. But then we have no idea what our work schedule, or bid line, will be for the following month until final bid awards are posted near the end of the current month.

The schedule can include any number of one to six-day trips, with any number of legs, meaning one flight of a multiflight trip. We could repeat the same trip each time or have a variety of different trips. For example, a bid line consisting of three-day trips could have three days on with three days off for one month. To maneuver days off, we can swap trips, as long as someone is willing to 'trip trade.'

It sounds like an auction. And it is. Once a month my life is auctioned off.

DING! Call light! Sorry about all the interruptions, but this is how my day goes. Be right back.

This call was the three UMs (unaccompanied minors) on board who had been constantly ringing their call buttons. One of them called to ask, "When are we going to be there?" Another one would do the same thing a few minutes later.

I answered both with, "I can assure you we're all ready to get there, too. Why don't you watch the movie or play with your iPad?"

The one in the middle turned upside down in his seat with his light-up tennis shoes up in the air. From his contorted-headstand position he asked, "Can I have another Coke?"

"You have to finish the Coke that I just brought a minute ago before you can have another one. OK?"

On one hand I felt sorry for these brothers, aged eight, nine, and ten, with all their bundled up energy ready to explode. On the other hand, a flight attendant can only offer so much. I saw movement under the tray table full of drinks as one of the boys foraged through the backpacks dumped out on the floor. Another flopped his body restlessly over his armrest and into the aisle, swinging his red hoodie like a matador at anyone who would give him attention.

Thankfully, the boys were located at a bulkhead-divider wall; at least that saved some poor souls from enduring the back of their seats being used as martial arts kicking bags the whole flight. Clearly bored, these kids should not have been traveling alone on a four-hour flight. Believe me, I took good care of them, but the price of their ticket didn't reflect how much time and attention a full-time babysitting service required.

Eventually, the boys learned not to be in love with the call button when another crew member told them, "You know, you can only ring the call button so many times, and then the window opens up and sucks you out."

OFF TO NEW YORK

Let me back up a little bit and fill you in on how I ended up in New York. After I finished initial flight attendant training at what is affectionately known as the *Charm Farm,* a hiring freeze due to the Gulf War kept me in suspense for six weeks. At last, I received the long-awaited phone call with my base assignment.

"You're going to New York."

"What? What about Raleigh-Durham?" *You know, near Cary, my hometown area.*

The realization hit me that everything in my life was about to change drastically along with all the challenges associated with relocating to New York. My mind raced, thinking of adjusting to life outside of marriage, a new job, and living in a new, big city all at the same time. The possibility of a new career based near my home was the only reason I'd followed my friend Anne's advice to apply for this job. Being at home might have helped to ease the burden of this turn-about in my life. This was supposed to be a simple transition into a new job. I guess not.

My elderly aunt lived in Manhasset, Long Island at the time, which was a convenient location to the New York airports. As soon as I got off the phone from hearing the exciting news, I called Aunt

Willa. The idea of me as a new roommate thrilled her. She'd been living in a spacious house by herself since my uncle passed away four years earlier. Her daughters tried to persuade her to move to a retirement community, but she wouldn't budge from where she'd been for the last forty-five years. We decided I'd live with her. This win-win situation worked out well for both of us.

Later, after hearing the horror stories about the accommodations of other new hires, I realized how good I had it. To save on expenses, they crowded as many newbie flight attendants as possible into whatever lodging they could find, all on short notice. The term 'Sardines' came up more than once. And with the clash of the mascara wands, as four to six women share one bathroom, Darth Vader wouldn't have stood a chance.

I really lucked out, not only was Nassau County, Long Island, the epitome of suburbia, but also, it was about a forty-five minute train ride into New York City (Manhattan) to go sightseeing. Along with its close proximity to the seventh largest city in the world, Willa's house was a commutable distance to LaGuardia and JFK (John F. Kennedy) airports. When I was young I always got Manhasset and Manhattan confused. Now I know that they were worlds apart.

I got settled into Aunt Willa's house, but we barely had time to chat and catch up on everything before I headed out the door for my first flight. It took me a few weeks to become acclimated to the area. I met lots of new people, in addition to running into my fellow classmates from the Charm Farm. It didn't take long before I officially succumbed to the unconventional lifestyle of a flight attendant.

PREFLIGHT

BE CAREFUL WHAT
YOU WISH FOR

It was never my lifelong dream to be a flight attendant. It never even crossed my mind. It happened by accident.

On that fateful day, I was having lunch with two of my best friends, Renea and Anne. Our conversations had covered all the bases: girl-talk, families, jobs, and curing any world crisis that came up. While venting about my boring job as a real estate appraiser, I said, "I wonder if there's some other profession that would take me away from all the paperwork and stressful deadlines."

Little did I know just how much of a sense of humor the job gods had when they decided to 'help.' I'd forgotten all about my wishful thinking until a week later when Anne showed up at my house and handed me an application form. She'd been a flight attendant for fifteen years with an airline that didn't have a crew base in our area. The long-distance commute made her job and her life miserable. So she brought me an application for the only airline with a local crew base.

"Elizabeth, don't throw this in the bottom of your slush pile. I know you too well." She gave me the stink-eye. "Fill this out. You never can tell what will happen."

"OK, OK. I will. I promise."

I thought one of the requirements for being a flight attendant was to be a dewy-eyed, twenty-something. As a not so dewy-eyed thirty-something, I didn't think I stood a chance and therefore didn't give it much thought. But since Anne had made the effort, I felt obliged to submit the application. I thought that would be the end of it.

A month later, when I went to my mailbox to get my bills and magazines, I found an innocuous envelope from the airline on the top of the pile. I took a deep breath and ripped it open.

They wanted me to come for an interview.

Oh shit, now what have I gotten myself into?

I didn't know the slightest thing about being a flight attendant. It's been said that ignorance is bliss, but I didn't know how blissful I was at the beginning of this adventure. If I knew then what I know now…I wouldn't have these stories to tell.

Nonetheless, my excitement mounted when I flew to the first interview at the airline's headquarters. One of the many recruiters escorted a group of twenty unsuspecting souls into a small room, where we sat on chairs in a circle. A perfectly groomed female airline representative, uniform spotless and every hair in place, sat down with a stack of papers in her lap. She began by saying; "I want each one of you to tell us something significant about yourself." I got the distinct impression the idea was to impress her with some difficult life situation we'd handled well. I was thinking back on my own history for what to say when she glanced to her left as a signal for the first person to begin.

A handsome man in a conservative suit stood up. "I've just been released from drug rehab. I've been clean for a month."

The interviewer almost fell off her folding chair as she drew a big "X" across the entire top sheet of his application. I later learned the FAA (Federal Aviation Administration) has a requirement for flight crews to have random drug tests to insure their zero-tolerance drug use policy. One down.

The process of weeding through the candidates had begun. The next wannabe flight attendant (F/A) stood up and said proudly, "I've just lost a hundred and fifty pounds." This achievement impressed me. The attractive blonde didn't look overweight, but my flight attendant friend, Anne, said this job was the worst for keeping a stable weight, with eating full meals on overnight flights at 2:00 or 3:00 o'clock in the morning and serving hot fudge sundaes three times a day on other flights. Not to mention that when a person is tired from an erratic sleep schedule they eat more due to a false impression it will provide a boost to that lost energy.

At that time, a fifty-year-old menopausal woman had to weigh the same as a twenty-year-old with no hormonal hot flashes. The only formula chart available used your height, which correlated to a designated weight. Flight attendants had to weigh in periodically in order to keep their jobs. No yo-yo diets allowed here. The interviewer gave her a big "X" as well. Two down.

Later, my friend Kathleen said that that applicant probably left there and ate the biggest hot-fudge sundae ever. I can't blame her. I've had some of those long days with three flights when I have been guilty of eating three hot-fudge-sundaes in one day. Hey, it's hard to resist the surplus ice cream left over and besides, I didn't want it to go to waste (or to waist).

I couldn't wait for the unusual-looking character next in line to enlighten us with his story. This guy, who looked too skinny to throw a shadow, was sporting a powder blue rented tuxedo with tails. I kid you not. That budding candidate said, in a baritone radio announcer's voice, "I love to talk on the microphone at McDonald's, because of that I know I'd make great announcements on the plane." I thought he had a good point, because most of the time I can't understand the garbled noise that comes out of either of them— McDonald's, or the airplane public address system (PA). His wide grin didn't save him and he got the next big "X." Three down.

Looking around the circle of strangers, I realized we all have circumstances that can lead to big "Xs" in our lives, some more so than others. With what I know now about the interview process, I definitely wouldn't have dared to tell a story like the one concerning what happened to me as a child growing up in the small town of Cary, North Carolina. When I was ten years old, my friend Renea (pronounced Renee) and I went out to the middle of a cow pasture in Kildaire Farms to retrieve my horse, Trigger. Evidently, the herd of cows didn't appreciate my taking their buddy away. They retaliated by stampeding directly toward us. I froze, paralyzed with fear, convinced I was about to die.

The fifty-some head of cattle charged full force, led by a massive bull. He zeroed in on me, the wide-eyed, scrawny little kid, as his target. I was going to be trampled to death. Just as we got eyeball-to-eyeball, he abruptly turned, leading his herd away. The onslaught of massive animals changed course so abruptly they kicked up dirt all over us. But when the dust settled, I realized that the fright-induced paralysis saved my life.

Did I mention that my brave friend Renea hid behind me?

I considered telling that story as an illustration of my skill in coping with stressful, fear-inducing situations – but after a few minutes, I concluded my story would also earn the big "X."

I decided to just keep parroting the people who didn't get an "X" - I love working with people, I love to travel, and I am flexible… *and remember to smile.* Yes, smile. *My cheeks hurt thinking about it.*

The main motivation for everyone at that interview was the travel benefits.

I did wonder if I was the only one who even thought about how to handle traumatic incidents without freezing. I looked around the room, wondering if anyone else might have this fight, flight, or freeze syndrome, or whatever psychological term would be used for a person who doesn't handle traumatic incidents very well. Now, as a seasoned flight attendant, I've been tested and I've proved that I can handle whatever catastrophic event might happen or fall out of the blue on an airplane.

When my turn came to share my accomplishments, I explained how I'd started a garden club in my neighborhood to help improve the community. I assured them that I was flexible, and I would be happy to move to any crew base they sent me to on short notice. And I smiled.

Each time we left a room, we were taken on a mystery tour, with a staff member telling us where to go. She pointed to me. "You go to the right, to the room at the end of the hall." Then to the next person, "You go to the left." I soon learned that the exit was on the left.

I went into the room and saw a girl I'd befriended earlier in the day. We were excited to see each other because this meant we'd both made it through the initial hurdles. "Boy," I said, "this is just like playing musical chairs. There are fewer people every go-around."

When I got home I called my friend Anne to tell her about the experience. "I made it through the interview, which seemed more like an audition. It was grueling." Anne laughed.

"And I'm tired of smiling."

"You should be happy. You made it through."

"I don't know what'll happen, but it made me feel like I accomplished something."

A few weeks went by and I tried not to think too much about it. Then I received the official letter. I got the job.

Now what do I do?

I was in the process of getting a divorce, so I figured that if a person was going to do the three most stressful things that can happen in a lifetime: divorce, change jobs and move - why not do them all at once and get it over with?

So, I got the divorce, changed my job, and moved to New York, all in the same year. Yes, I blasted off from my southern hometown, Cary, North Carolina to New York City—by way of Long Island where I lived for a couple of years.

In this process, I discovered I'm a magnet for bizarre incidents, on the ground as well as in mid-air. Here are some tales of the strange, the unexplained, and the downright weird from my world as a flight attendant. These tales include dead bodies in garment bags, roosters, sex, and nudity on the plane. All these things have really happened—to me, or to my flying buddies, during my twenty-some years working with the airline.

Every life is a journey. Being a flight attendant takes that proverb a step further, to a literal translation. Every day on the job is both a journey and an adventure, some days more so than others.

So if you've had a hard day at work and need to escape your 'on the ground' job, put on your seat belt and join me at 35,000 feet.

I SHOULD HAVE LISTENED TO MY MOTHER

Now that you're familiar with my schedule, come along as a stowaway with me to witness a normal day in my life as a flight attendant.

A typical day... actually, there is no typical day, so just tag along.

"I can't be late for sign in," I mumbled to myself, as I hurried through the busy airport. Now, I'm trying to get through these people without bopping someone over the head with my plastic water bottle. That's my road rage showing through. But not on the road, I'm talking about in the airport. Does anyone else get road rage walking behind slow people?

The obstacle course ahead of me was slowing me down on my mission to arrive at flight attendant operations a few minutes early. It seems like when I'm in a hurry even the smallest family can take up huge spaces. I dodged through the crowds of slow-moving people, swerved around a newlywed couple holding hands, squeezed through extended families with baby strollers, while deflecting around window shoppers. That's when I spotted John, a pilot friend of mine from North Carolina, who waved at me from across the terminal.

We were both moving at a fast pace, doing the roller-bag race through the airport. When we got closer, John said, "You won't believe what happened on my flight."

He looked all keyed-up, as he came to an abrupt stop right in front of me. His heavy tote bag, hitched on the back of his rollaboard suitcase, hit the ground with a thud.

I loved his stories so I egged him on, even though I didn't have a lot of time to spare. "What happened?"

"Aw man, I just came in from a turnaround trip to Guatemala. But before we left Miami, I was walking up to the plane when I spotted a huge Latin family all standing right in front of the gate consoling each other. You've never seen so much wailing and crying and carrying on. It was prior to boarding, so no one was going to get past these people to board the plane."

"What was that all about?" I know we don't want a whole bunch of upset passengers on an airplane. John took off his uniform hat and smoothed down a lock of brown hair. He pointed across the terminal to the wall-to-wall crowd ready for boarding. "There were more people than that, and everyone just stood back away from the family giving them space, like they had the plague or something."

"That's so bizarre."

He lowered his voice. "I high-tailed it straight to the agent behind the counter to find out what on earth was going on. Well, turns out this family had come to Miami to escort the body of their beloved Uncle José, who'd died in Puerto Rico, to his final resting place in Guatemala. But guess what? Uncle José didn't make the flight from San Juan!"

"Uncle José missed his own funeral?" I gasped. "Really? He really missed his own funeral? Don't tell me his casket is lost."

John nodded his head. Yeah, I guess eventually whoever is in charge of lost luggage will find him and send him home.

"I've heard that saying---You're going to miss your own funeral---my whole life. That's what my mama used to tell me every time I was running late, which was often.

I shook my head in disbelief. "Never in my wildest dreams would I have thought it could actually happen to someone. My mother was right as usual."

I should've listened to my mother.

ANOTHER GLORIOUS DAY ON A TYPICAL FLIGHT ATTENDANT TRIP

Man, I barely slid into home plate. I remember this as being my normal procedure back then, just making it on time into the flight attendant operations room, affectionately known as Ops. The room bustled with crew members of various shapes, sizes, and ages all signing in, checking duty schedules, and printing out airline information. Noise blared from a cacophony of conversations, last minute phone calls, and humming printers. I scanned the maze of counters, desperate for an available computer terminal so I could sign in. Finally, I squeezed into a free spot and signed in for my trip. Then I made my way to the gate where I met my fellow crew members.

Another flight attendant came running up. "Hi everybody, I'm Susan. I'm on reserve. Crew schedule just called me out for this trip two hours ago because somebody called in sick. Or something else could have happened to him. I don't know."

I wondered if the absent person had caught the new epidemic going around, known as *Anal Glaucoma*, (I can't *see* my *ass* going to work today.)

I gave Scott, the purser (lead flight attendant), a quick hug. I'd flown with him before and knew he was easy to work with, always polite and went out of his way to help everyone. As for the rest of the crew, they were a whole new crop of faces.

We gathered around Scott, our fearless leader, for updates on the flight, as he looked through the paperwork he'd just received from the agent.

"The cleaners are on the plane now. As soon as we can go on board, the captain wants to have a briefing."

Today should be the usual routine, so I wasn't expecting anything out of the norm but we always have to be on our toes. After the plane had been cleaned, restocked, and inspected, we boarded, put our bags away, did our security and emergency equipment checks, and gathered for our preflight security briefing. The captain, Mike Johnson, came out of the cockpit, introduced himself and discussed issues likely to impact the flight, such as weather, turbulence, and maintenance problems.

After Mike had finished, Scott said, "Watch out for the passengers who have started their vacations a little too early, either with the little umbrella drinks or something stronger. Keep a look out for any kind of disturbance that might be a problem and here's another new kicker – domestic violence. Did you hear about the incident last week when a plane had to make an emergency landing because some newlywed couple got into a fistfight?"

We all cracked up laughing, then the jokes started.

I asked Scott, "What was the title of the news report? 'Married bliss on the couple's flight to jail.'"

I thought of some more titles. "How about, 'Handcuffed on their honeymoon and fettered forever' or 'The bonds of their love chains on planes.'"

Someone else said, "I've heard that matrimony is a wonderful institution but who wants to be in an institution for the rest of your life?"

Another crew member said, "That puts a new twist on make-up sex if you're already in handcuffs."

Scott looked at his watch. "Ok, move it, here come the passengers. Let the games begin."

We darted to our respective work positions and the boarding process began with the always hectic, drama-filled theatrics of getting the passengers seated as quickly as possible for an on-time departure.

I expected the usual situations that crop up where people require my help. For example, people leave their computers or purses in the security checkpoint or misplace their boarding passes, cell phones, passports, or loved ones. I've always been puzzled as to how someone could leave a purse or wallet in the security checkpoint, but it happens.

We're all conditioned to spot the look of panic from quite a distance. If you've ever seen the movie, *Home Alone,* you might remember the scene when the mother screamed out, "Kevin?" I've seen that look many times.

On this flight a man couldn't locate his passport and while throwing an accusatory look at everyone around him, he swore that someone had stolen it. While standing in the middle of the aisle blocking the flow of passengers, he started yelling and flailing his arms in all directions. Another flight attendant discovered the passport in the row in front of his seat. Evidently, he had set it down while putting his bags in the overhead bin.

A couple of rows forward of that scene, a lady demanded everyone remove their bags from *her* overhead bin because it was full. I explained that the overhead bin is shared space and she should head toward any open bin further back.

Next, a lady with a small child whose facial expression told it all. Their seats were separated and tears streamed down the cheeks of the little girl. The mother asked the gentleman next to her if he would kindly trade seats. He refused.

Overhearing this conversation I jumped in, "Sir, that is perfectly fine but I'm going to pull out this barf bag in her seatback pocket for you... Do you mind holding this for her, she's not feeling well. I see you have a handkerchief, pointing to his pocket square. If we hit any kind of turbulence you'll need some more paper towels. I will get you some as soon as everyone is seated."

He patted his pocket square on his expensive suit while the wheels turned in his head. In two seconds he jumped up and asked the mother for the seat number.

Flight attendants have to be ingenious and ready to handle anything that comes up. And I do mean anything.

NOW BOARDING

LET THE STAMPEDE BEGIN!

Definition: Stampede

1. A sudden frenzied rush of panic-stricken animals.

2. A sudden headlong rush or flight of a crowd of people.

Did you know the ultimate goal of an airline is an on-time departure? To accomplish this the door of the airplane should be closed ten minutes early. This can only happen with all passengers seated, and all overhead bins shut, totally prepared for the departure. Just for your information, airlines recently changed this from ten minutes to closing the door to fifteen minutes early. And what this means to you, dear passenger, is… Please don't be late. All luggage properly stowed means no big duffle bag on a passenger's lap or an oversized bag, the size of a Volkswagen, shoved between the seats on the floor. Those passengers are easy to spot with their feet propped on top and their knees stuck up in the air.

These passengers are always the ones who stare at me like I have three heads and say, "I don't see why my bag can't stay here?" *REeeaLLY, are you going to be comfortable in that contorted position for hours on end?*

I gesture toward the person seated next to the window to explain. "How's your seatmate going to get out in the event of an emergency? That's why there's an FAA regulation that carry-on luggage must fit entirely under the seat in front of you. Did you know in an emergency evacuation we're trained to get three hundred people off the airplane in ninety seconds? You think about that one for a minute – or a minute and a half."

I let this information sink in for a second because what people don't know is there are about two hundred evacuations a year. And these involve some of the same people – the ones who take forever to saunter on to the plane, then stand in the middle of the aisle and take their sweet time to unpack all their belongings out of each bag before getting settled into their seats.

As the #4 flight attendant on this flight, I helped the agents check tickets at the gate. Lately, to cut costs, the airline has eliminated food and the extra flight attendant so we have only minimum crew on board.

But on that day the drama started when I spotted an elderly couple running from the other end of the terminal, wildly waving their arms and yelling, "Don't leave us!"

The silver-haired man arrived first, huffing, and puffing, his arms over-loaded with their coats and carry-on bags.

Trying to be sympathetic, I asked, "Did you have to run from another connecting flight?"

However, before her husband could make up an excuse, the out-of-breath wife, still running toward the gate blurted out, "No. We ran from the bar. We almost had one Mai Tai too many."

I didn't have to say anything. My raised eyebrows said it all. I just followed these two, last to board passengers down the jet bridge and helped them find their seats.

Back on board, a disgruntled older businessman seated toward the front of coach said, "You won't believe what happened to me."

Before I could reply or run to the other end of the airplane he confronted me with every fray that had happened to him the whole week. He pointed his finger at me as if everything was my fault.

When I thought he was winding down, he shifted into high gear. "Isn't there another seat? I don't like this one. Why isn't the overhead space larger? This flight is going to be delayed, isn't it? Are there any first class seats available?" He didn't wait for an answer.

I listened to his rants and raves, which had absolutely nothing to do with me. This disgruntled man was gunning for someone to take his aggression out on. He found his captive audience, and unfortunately, I was his target.

Every time I closed the overhead bin, he got up to dig something else out of his bag and left the bin open. After this happened several times, I told another crew member to beware of the problem passenger in aisle seat 11C.

This tall, fit-looking male flight attendant happened to have a black belt in karate. I thought my fellow colleague planned to just follow me back up the aisle past this man to get a look at Mr. Squeaky Wheel. But he had other plans. With lightning precision, my Kung Fu crew member took a flying front kick to shut the overhead bin.

He reached a height of at least seven feet straight up in the air and yelled "Heeee-ya!" as he shut the overhead bin above the man's head with his foot.

My mouth dropped open from my viewpoint standing a few rows right in front of this high-flying display. I quickly regained my composure and hid the shock on my face.

The passenger took on an expression of surprised nervousness, hunching his shoulders and sliding down in his seat as he viewed the not-so-humble flight attendant with a newfound respect.

My crew member then said to him, "Sir, can I help you with anything else?" in a 'make my day' tone of voice.

"No…uh…thank you."

This man didn't bother us again for the rest of the flight.

I thought the worst was over, as the boarding process continued at a snail's pace, when a female passenger in the aft (rear) section started screaming. The flight attendant setting up the aft galley ran out to check out the disturbance. She arrived just in time to see a young man pulling up his pants in the middle of the aisle.

The story we got later was the young man had been 'styling,' - wearing pants so low that he was exhibiting most of his underwear. The very large woman seated in the aisle seat had refused to stand up to let the young man pass to his seat. This forced him to try to squeeze in between her plus-sized legs already pushed against the forward seatback. He crawled over her and helplessly trampled on her feet in an attempt to get to his assigned seat. Caught in the tight squeeze, his pants could not take any added pressure and the tug brought everything down. In this embarrassing moment, he had both his arms clutched around his backpack as the woman got an eyeful that wasn't included in the ticket price.

That's when the screaming started. He threw his backpack down, corrected his wardrobe malfunction, and jumped back into the aisle to escape the screeching woman. The astonished flight attendant emerged to catch the tail end, grand finale, of the strip-tease act.

The commotion didn't end there on this packed flight. The flight attendant now had to ask several passengers if they would trade their seats to accommodate the woman because she refused to sit next to the amateur stripper.

She loudly proclaimed, "I've already seen enough of him for one flight!"

But the best was still to come. In the middle of the action, the caterer came in the front door with an additional oven rack of meals to be taken to the aft galley. F/A Mark took the long skinny metal tray, about a foot wide and three feet long, full of entrees, from the caterer. Holding it out in front of him, he carefully maneuvered his way down the narrow aisle. Like a bumper-car, Mark made his way through the passengers, nudging elbows and shoulders on each side. He'd almost lost his balance a few times on this precarious obstacle course, while stumbling over feet and bags invisible to him below the load he was gripping tight with both hands.

Along the way, a male passenger leaned over into the aisle to retrieve something out of his bag on the floor. Mark kept on walking a few more feet, but he was bewildered by the unidentified, hairy object hanging on the end of the tray. He finally figured out the corner of the oven tray had snatched the toupee right off the leaning man's head. When Mark figured out what had happened, all he could do was back up the aisle, with the man's toupee still dangling on the end, to return the bald man's hairpiece to him with an apology. "Oops!"

Elizabeth Calwell

LIONS, TIGERS and BEARS ALONG WITH MUGGERS and MURDERERS...OH MY!

My new life as a flight attendant took some adjusting to, not just on the airplane itself, but in my home life, too. Case in point, living on Long Island, New York with my aunt, I learned about her eccentricities as well as those of her friends. Aunt Willa had lots of friends and/ or "partners in crime" who lassoed me into being the designated driver for their luncheon gatherings. Not because of alcohol, as no one drank at lunch. My chauffeur duties made it convenient for the women to get together in new places, because they didn't like to drive outside the comfort zone of their local area.

On one occasion, we were going to an Italian restaurant a couple of towns over from Manhasset. It wasn't very far because on Long Island every stoplight you come to is another town.

Aunt Willa was ready to go—on time, as always. She was dressed in a pair of casual slacks, a white tunic-shirt, and a white sweater. She always wore a wrap or sweater because no matter where she sat in the restaurant, she felt a breeze from the air conditioner. She kind-of reminded me of Betty White in her favorite beauty parlor turned out hairdo she had maintained for the last thousand years. She even had the same candy-kid dimples with just as big a smile as the movie star. I threw myself together at the last second – pants with a nice shirt, slapped on a necklace and I was ready to go.

This was my first meeting with this group of Willa's friends and I have to admit I was apprehensive at the idea of going out to lunch with four ladies, all of whom were almost twice my age. But it turned out to be fun. I enjoyed driving beside the scenic waterfront on Long Island, and exploring the different locations as we picked up my Aunt Willa's friends.

Naomi lived closest so she was first. She was a shopaholic and because she lived around the corner from Aunt Willa, she became my shopping buddy...or perhaps it was the other way around. At times it was difficult to tell.

As she settled in the back seat of Willa's big Buick, I couldn't help but notice her blouse, patterned with bright orange and greenish-blue swirls. She may have been a few years younger than Aunt Willa, but she only dressed in the latest trends.

I greeted her. "Hello Naomi, I like your shirt."

She cocked her head to one side as she flipped her collar up.

"Got it at my favorite hangout, Filene's Basement." She said this with a big smile, then shifted right into gossip mode.

"Did you see in the news about 'the Love Triangle' right here in Nassau County? Oh my, and that poor wife got shot by the girlfriend. What's that monstrosity our neighbor is building on the side of his house? Whew, it's hot today."

Naomi fanned her face without taking a breath or a pause in between her unconnected sentences. I could forget about getting another word in edgewise from then on.

This robust personality chattered non-stop, her mane of red hair bouncing as she laughed, finding humor in everything. Willa, Naomi, and I picked up the other two ladies, Mary Ann and Ethel, then headed for DiMaggio's restaurant in Port Washington to meet up with Pat.

Mary Ann said, "You're going to love this place. The last time we were here the owner sang opera to us. He really enjoys mingling with the customers, and the food is delicious."

These ladies had lived here forever. On the way to the restaurant they provided me with inside information on where to find the rich and famous. Naomi pointed to a large estate with a circular driveway.

"A Mafia Don lives there."

"How do you know that? Isn't that scary?" I said as I glanced at Naomi through the rear view mirror. "I don't know anything about the Mafia except what I've seen in movies like *The Godfather*."

"We went in there and checked it out," Ethel said. "That was when they were first building it."

"Until they hired security guards to keep us out." Naomi couldn't hold back her enthusiasm. "Before that happened we saw them put in three different hidden walls and a big safe in the basement."

"How do you know it was a hidden wall?"

I just couldn't picture these ladies sneaking around checking out anything involved with the Mafia.

"Because the whole wall swiveled," Ethel said. "They were building secret compartments. We couldn't figure out what the heck it was until Naomi leaned on one accidentally and it moved. That's when we got kicked out."

"Mary Ann," said Ethel, "tell everybody about what happened to Anthony at the dry cleaners."

"Oh yeah. Anthony is a good friend of mine. He told me the other day that Mikey the Fish, what's his name - I forget his last name - anyway he took his suit in to have it dry cleaned. Guess what they found in the pocket? Eighteen thousand dollars! My friend, Anthony, put the money in a paper bag and took it back into his office. He was torn between telling Mikey or keeping the money for himself in the hope that Mikey wouldn't remember it, when the phone rang.

"Mikey the Fish said in a heavy accent, 'Antney, I left twenty large in the pocket of my coat.'"

"Holy shit. What did Antney, I mean Anthony, do?" Naomi asked.

"I bet he shit a brick thinking he was going to have to cough up another two thousand," Willa added her two-cents in.

"I think he did," Mary Ann said, "but he swore to Mikey that there was only eighteen thousand there and I guess the Fish Man believed him because Anthony is still alive."

Willa changed the subject, pointing to another house. "And that's where Frances Hodgson Burnett lived when she wrote *The Secret Garden.*"

Then they showed me a road leading to where John Philip Sousa had lived. Sousa marches always reminded me of watching the fireworks on the Fourth of July.

"Wow. Y'all have tons of famous people right around here."

Lunch was seasoned with fascinating conversation, including discussions of rape and murder cases from Pat, the retired lawyer in the group. Not the typical lunch gossip I'd imagined with these women.

These well-informed ladies kept me up to date with the latest current events I might have missed while out of the country. In return, I told stories from my airline travels. I became a new source of entertainment for Willa and her friends.

Our first lunchtime conversation, as the new person living in New York, they focused on my safety. *Uh oh!*

These ladies indoctrinated me with enough instructions on New York safety precautions to have me ready for any assault that might be coming my way. But it was good advice.

"For example," Ethel said, as she reached into her huge purse and emptied handfuls of her important essentials out onto the table, obviously trying to find something valuable in the bottomless cavern, "when pulling up to a red light, always leave enough space between you and the car in front. This keeps you from being pinned in and allows room to maneuver in the event of a car-jacking or an assault by gang members."

She added another handful of pill bottles and receipts to the pile of debris on the table. "These crimes are all over the news every night." She said all of this in a matter-of-fact tone, without looking up, as she was still concentrating on getting to the bottom of her bag. "Ah, found 'em." She slid her reading glasses on.

Another one of the lunch bunch, Mary Ann, added her advice while pointing her index finger at me.

"Lock all your car doors, and don't leave your windows down either. My friend Alice was waiting for a red light to change when a man just reached in and grabbed her purse. She fought with him but he was too strong."

I had just returned from a Los Angeles trip, so I shared a conversation I'd had with a passenger on the plane.

"Hey, speaking of horrible crimes, there was a Detroit police officer on my flight last night. We started talking about a Northwest flight attendant who was murdered in her hotel room on a layover. He was the prime investigator."

Since this story broke in the middle of my initial training I was well aware of the details. Depictions of what happened went through the airline community like wildfire. It scared us all to death, especially the bright-eyed, unseasoned new hires who had no idea of what to expect with our new career choice.

Willa said, "This doesn't put a good light on your new job."

"Yeah, I know, but that conversation with him will be etched in my memory forever. Sorry, I guess this isn't exactly something to talk about while eating."

But as I looked around the table their expectant faces prompted me to continue with the officer's vivid, first-hand account.

"He and his partner were the first ones on the crime scene. Not holding back any of the gory details, he said the flight attendant must have fought like crazy. The room was wrecked, and covered with blood. He said it was the worst butchery he'd ever seen...and what was baffling was there were no signs of forced entry."

"So how did the guy get in?" Pat asked, raising her eyebrows.

"That's exactly what I'd like to know. That's the part that scares the shit outta me, especially after what happened to my friend, Anne."

"Anne and Elizabeth have been best friends since they were little," Willa said. "She's also the flight attendant that got Elizabeth into this mess or, should I say, dangerous career. You know, with friends like that, who needs enemies?" Everyone laughed and nodded.

Willa always spoke her mind so I braced for whatever she might say next. "So what happened to Anne? I hope she wasn't hurt. If that's the case, then you're just going to have to find another, less glamorous, job."

"Well, Anne told me, as the newbie flight attendant, what I should do when I go into a hotel room. You know she's a calloused veteran of some twenty-years. She gave me the security lecture because of what happened to her on one of her first trips."

"Tell us about it," the ladies said.

"I can still picture Anne, with the intense expression in her dark brown eyes, saying 'Every single time—and I do mean every time—you go into a hotel room, you check it out first.' "

"Her crew had arrived at the layover hotel and had decided to meet back in the lobby as soon as possible to go out to dinner. Trying not to be late, Anne dropped her bags as soon as she entered the hotel room, threw her purse on the bed, and got into the shower. When she came out of the bathroom, the door had been unlocked and her wallet was gone. The guy was hiding in the room when she came in. Thank heavens all he wanted was her money.

"Anne's warning has stuck with me forever. When I enter a hotel room, I always check behind the curtains and shower curtain, under the bed, in the closet, and anywhere else someone could hide."

After recounting this piece of advice to the ladies, I got another word of wisdom from Mary Ann, the elder of the luncheon group.

"When walking down a street in New York, or any big city, keep a few one-dollar bills in your pocket, so that you'll have them ready if you encounter a robber. Throw the money, then run like hell in the opposite direction. The mugger just wants money, not a confrontation."

I tried not to laugh out loud while mulling over the mental image of an eighty-year-old lady, with skinny legs and granny shoes, holding up her skirt with one hand and her hat with the other *running like hell*. It turned out this recommendation really came in handy later when I moved into New York City.

All of these suggestions came as a surprise to me. But there were more surprises in store in my New York life.

LEARNING ABOUT NEW YORK

Moving to Long Island proved to be an interesting change of pace. In North Carolina I grew up in a house where we never even locked the front door. More and more my new life resembled *The Wizard of Oz*, because I was definitely not in Kansas (or North Carolina) anymore.

I soon learned my way around, and my little car, named "Squeaky," took me wherever I needed to go. My mechanic in N.C. had given my Toyota Corolla hatchback that nickname. A squeak in the engine drove him crazy because he couldn't find the source of the unusual noise. The squeak never seemed to affect how the car drove; so we just let well enough alone, and I learned to live with it.

The stress of flying was nothing compared to driving. All flight attendants based in New York covered all three airports: LaGuardia, JFK, and Newark. Leaving for work at three or four o'clock in the morning became a typical routine along with often coming home well after midnight.

I learned to drive defensively in New York. This meant racing along at a speed of at least eighty to eighty-five miles per hour just to keep up with the rest of the crazy drivers.

Squeaky and I always took the same route, clinging to the main roads. Veering even one block over would have taken me into dangerous neighborhoods, unsafe in the day or night. And I never let the gas tank fall below the half-full mark in case of an unexpected detour or traffic jam.

If a person left their broken-down car on the side of the road, even for a short period of time, they could return to a shell of a vehicle sitting up on concrete blocks. This was a common sight. I never thought about abandoning Squeaky because these car-stripping gangs could cannibalize a car in four to eight minutes.

A New Yorker once told me the story of a man who developed car trouble and pulled his vehicle over on the shoulder of the road. He hitched a ride to an auto supply store and came back with a new radiator hose to fix the leak. While leaning over the engine in the front with the hood propped up and the traffic whizzing by, he didn't notice when a car screeched to a halt behind him. A couple of guys jumped out and started jacking up his car.

He yelled at them, "What the @#$% are you doing?"

They yelled back, "It's okay buddy. We only want the tires. You can have the battery."

MY FIRST DAY AS AN INTERNATIONAL
FLIGHT ATTENDANT

Just when I had become accustomed to driving to LaGuardia, the domestic crew base, my transfer came through as an international flight attendant, now based out of JFK.

At first I didn't want to transfer into international because I thought I would be required to wear a hat.

I'd asked a colleague once, while watching another flight attendant walk by, why the woman was wearing a hat.

"Oh, she's international," she answered matter-of-factly. Same thing happened again, on a different day, as another flight attendant walked by wearing a hat. With my inexperience I wasn't aware that these were the only two flight attendants who wore hats. All I could think about was 'hat hair.'

No way, I don't want to be international. I didn't think at all about the dangers of being in a foreign country, language barriers, health issues with ionized radiation exposure on longer flights, higher expenses, strange food, and no phone calls, much less the aggravation of having to clear customs each trip. Nope, just *hat hair.*

But one day, when I shared a seat on the crew bus with a captain, I changed my mind. I asked him about his trip.

He said, "I'm so sick of that Crabtree Valley Mall."

I perked up at the sound of something familiar to me in North Carolina.

"That's one of my favorite malls in Raleigh. You're international. Why would you go there?"

"We go from JFK to Bermuda and then on to Raleigh to layover."

"You're kidding!" Now my wheels were turning… a Raleigh layover, I would only be a few miles from my hometown of Cary.

I immediately signed up for the proffer (transfer) and I got it. I lucked out because up until then only the most senior flight attendants, who we call senior mamas, could hold the international division of the airline. Normally, flying out of the country was out of reach for someone as super junior as me with only three months of flying under my belt. In the seniority scale I would've been considered a toddler.

Later I found out that the two senior mamas who wore the hats did so only as a symbol of the longevity of their careers; they'd been working for forty years or more. Hats were no longer issued as part of the uniform. Once again, all I could think of were the problems of dealing with a hat. Nowhere to store it on a packed airplane, or wearing a hat in one hundred degree temperatures with humidity. And I would be afraid, with my luck, I would probably forget it somewhere or drop it in a toilet.

I have always been a major procrastinator. In all my excitement of getting packed and ready for my first international sign-in early the next morning at a new airport (JFK), I waited too late to paint my fingernails. I thought a good plan of action would be to paint my nails before I left in the car so they would have an hour to dry on the way.

My mother always had gorgeous painted fingernails, and frankly, I don't know how she did it. But now I'm trying to figure it out because this job required me to have painted nails.

As a new hire on probation we often had grooming checks. I didn't need to be late this morning and had run out of time, so I only painted a few of my nails, and headed out, thinking I could finish at a stoplight.

You never get a red light when you need one. So, I tried a quick 'bat turn' into what I thought was a neighborhood but it turned out to be a gated community. With nowhere to turn around I drove up to the guardhouse.

"Sir, excuse me. I'm sorry to wake you up but I need to finish painting my nails."

I held up all my fingernails to show him the four bright red nails on one hand.

"Whatever."

He yawned as he opened the gate so I would be able to turn around instead of backing out into the traffic. He probably thought he'd now seen everything. I finished painting my nails, but lost more time before pulling back onto the main highway.

I merged onto the freeway at eighty-five miles per hour, hoping I could make up some time. Without warning, a truckload of telephone cabling spools came unfastened from a large utility vehicle right in front of me. The giant spools resembled spinning tops as they bounced off the back of the truck and spun erratically out of control across the beltline. Cars, trucks, and buses scattered in all directions, like bumper cars, as the rush hour traffic dodged the unpredictable airborne objects. Just one of those spools could have taken out my little car. It happened so fast that all my instincts to react took over as I swerved through them like a NASCAR driver.

Miraculously, Squeaky and I made it through unscathed. Shaken, but not stirred.

Finally at the airport, I dropped off my bags in the crew storage area just inside operations and searched for an available computer. I slid in between two other crew members.

In my haste, I turned to a redheaded captain standing slightly more than an elbow distance away, and asked, "Do you know if this computer works? This is my first trip out of JFK, and at LaGuardia some of the computers don't work. I'm really in a hurry this morning."

"It should work. Someone else just finished using it."

I proceeded to type. Wouldn't you know the stupid computer wouldn't let me sign in? *Haven't I been through enough for one day?*

"Oh shoot! What now?"

The pilot couldn't help but notice my exasperation as he finished folding up his flight plan printouts, and he offered to help.

"You have to type in this code. The last person pulled up a different screen. It should work now."

"Whew! I made it. Thank you so much. I'm off to my first international trip to Santo Domingo."

I gathered up my paperwork and rushed to the gate.

After finishing the breakfast service, several of the flight attendants gathered in the galley. A woman approached and tapped me on the shoulder.

"You need to do something about that rooster."

I glanced at my colleagues for some guidance; *somebody help me out here, I don't know what she's talking about.*

Lightheartedly, I replied, "Hey, I'm the junior flight attendant here. I don't do roosters." *I honestly thought she was joking.*

We all laughed because we thought we'd misunderstood what she said.

Raising her voice, she said, "I'm not kidding. You need to do something about that rooster. It's waking up my baby."

By this time a few more flight attendants had joined us. We all went to investigate. There it was – a rooster. A man had snuck it on board in a brown-paper bag then shoved it under the seat in front of him, just as he had been instructed to do in the safety demonstration. It's just that the safety demo referred to small carry-on bags, not live farm animals. And do you know what a rooster does when it wakes up? It crows a piercingly loud, "Cock-a-doodle-doo." Repeatedly.

Passengers started waking up, confused about the source of the noise. When they realized that it really was a live rooster, most of them started laughing.

One of our senior mamas said, "Oh yeah, years ago, quite often we would have to break up cock fights on the plane. There would be feathers flying everywhere."

"You've got to be kidding."

"Of course, the airlines didn't condone it. Some passengers just decided they would make the flight a little more exciting by adding their own entertainment."

"What are we going to do with this rooster?" one of the crew asked the purser.

"I guess we're going to leave it where it is. I mean, what else can we do?"

The rooster finally quieted down.

I went to the back of the plane and had just sat down on an empty jump seat when the inter-phone rang. A senior flight attendant answered it and turned to me.

"Elizabeth, the captain wants to see you in the cockpit, immediately."

"Why does he want to talk to me?" *I don't think I did anything wrong. No captain has ever called me to come to the cockpit before. I don't even know these pilots.* "What does he want?"

"I don't know. That's all he said."

I really didn't know the procedure because in the three short months that I'd been flying I'd only been in the cockpit a couple of times.

The galley flight attendant in the front said, "Just walk on in."

There on the left side sat the redheaded captain from operations.

"Hey, you helped me sign in this morning," I said with relief at the sight of a friendly face.

"Thank you so much for your help. I'm Elizabeth." I reached out to shake his hand.

Elizabeth Calwell

"I'm Gary and this is Steve." He pointed to the first officer. "Don't you know those computers in Ops don't work when you're in a hurry?"

"You've got that right," I replied as I surveyed the tiny area. Buttons, switches, toggles, gauges, dials, knobs, and instruments covered every inch of overhead and wall space. "Wow! How do you know what all these gizmos are for? No way in hell I would ever try to fly one of these birds."

"This plane has digital fly-by-wire technology. Its computer technology can practically fly itself."

The first officer finished moving dials and writing down numbers as he removed his headset.

"Yeah, but they still need us in case of an emergency. We have over a hundred checks in the cockpit besides walking around the outside of the plane before each takeoff."

They both proceeded to show me the CliffsNotes version of the cockpit, as well as how to land the plane if I needed to.

"Yeah right, like that's going to ever happen." Somehow visions of myself as some sort of Rambo hero landing the aircraft just didn't fit with my job description.

"Elizabeth, you could land this plane."

"Nope, not me."

"No, I'm serious," said Gary. "The computer system can detect radio signals from the ground to land the plane. Anyway, since this is your first Airbus flight I thought you might like to see the cockpit."

"No thank you," I said, shaking my head. "I don't want to know anything about landing a plane. You just get me on the ground safely, and I'll be very grateful."

I'd read those stories in *Readers Digest* about people who had to land the plane when something happened to the pilot. Nope, not me. I don't ever want to be in that predicament.

As I turned to leave I said, "I know you called me up here as an initiation of the newbie flight attendant but thanks for showing me around. It's been a pleasure to meet you two."

Fortunately, nothing traumatic happened that required me to land the plane. And besides giving me a heart attack for thinking I was in trouble, the pilots just wanted to explain things to me, just in case. So I lived through my first international trip … roosters and all.

THE COMMUTE FROM HELL

This trip qualified me as the commuter from hell. This awful day started with getting up at 3:30 in the morning trying to get back to New York from Raleigh. Storms on the east coast caused me to be bumped off full flights all day long starting with the first one at 6 a.m. Since I fly standby, no empty seat means I don't get on the plane. My only choice to head north was to fly into Newark, New Jersey.

With no clue about Newark airport, I didn't have the slightest idea how difficult the process would be to get from there to JFK airport where my car sat in the parking lot. Going home to North Carolina was refreshing. But getting back to New York, to Aunt Willa's house on Long Island and my job, was not only problematic but in fact, it turned into the commute from hell.

After I arrived in Newark, a policeman told me, "Take a bus into New York City; then change to a bus to JFK. That's the only way to get there by bus. Yuz can take a taxi. It's faster but it will cost you a small fortune."

That sounds like going way around my elbow to get somewhere. But I didn't have time to think about it.

"Quick! There's your bus." Another woman trying to be helpful pointed at a bus loading up. "It's leaving for the City in two minutes. You'll be at the bus stop close to Grand Central."

Taking her advice, I jumped on the bus just in the nick of time. I ended up in NYC standing at the curb in the middle of a block. I didn't see Grand Central Station anywhere and I didn't know all the buses had already quit running for the day.

Now, how did I get myself into this mess?

It was now midnight. I kept looking at my watch, as I stood at the New York City bus stop in the dark for over an hour – by myself. I knew this wide vacant area was the right spot because I'd positioned myself next to the signpost for JFK airport. A cell phone would've come in handy but this was pre-cell phone days. With no knowledge about the city or the transportation system, I didn't have any other alternative. I was afraid if I walked away I would miss the bus. But with no one around to ask for information, this spooky situation kept getting spookier by the minute.

The midnight hour had come and gone. Minutes ticked away as I stood there alone, consumed by the feeling of being helpless prey waiting for God-knows-what to happen. If you haven't ever been stranded alone in a big city in a neighborhood you don't recognize with people moving around you who are staring at you with that creepy feeling going up the back of your neck – well, good for you.

The stories drilled into me by the well-meaning natives brought the dire consequences of this situation even more to light. A single female standing alone at night was not only in danger, but the situation could become deadly. I'd put myself in harm's way and didn't dare make eye contact or talk to the few strange-looking characters out so late.

I'd never seen homeless people before. Why would anyone be out wandering around at this hour? They made me feel even more apprehensive. One woman wearing multiple layers of ill-fitted, mismatched clothes topped off with a dirty, knitted, stocking cap slowly hobbled past, pushing all her dumpster-diving treasures piled high on a stolen shopping cart. Some people appeared more eccentric than others as they shuffled along in worn-out tennis shoes four sizes too big, and heavy wool coats, not necessary in the mild weather.

Everything about them painted a picture of a dismal life. I smelled the stench of poverty and despair and felt their stares. As I glanced around, the ones who weren't toting grocery carts were staring at me, probably thinking the same thing. 'What's that nicely dressed woman doing out here? She must not have better sense than to be out on the streets alone this late at night.'

I had to agree.

I prayed that some desperate, drugged-out lunatic wouldn't bother me.

What will I do if I'm assaulted? Mentally I prepared for fight or flight, and then I spotted a grungy-looking man coming straight toward me. His clothes hung loosely on his hunched-over, skeletal body. Through his disheveled, long, stringy hair I saw his dark eyes fixed right on me.

Oh Lord. Let me live through this one. Maybe if I don't look scared he'll go away.

Please keep on walking. Please keep on walking.

The nefarious homeless guy continued coming. Getting closer.

Okay, get ready. I took in a deep breath as my body tensed. I glanced in his direction…still coming, straight at me.

All of a sudden, a big city bus appeared from around the corner and pulled up in front of me. The driver opened the door and, barking in a New York accent, he said, "Why are you standing there?"

"Someone told me this was the bus stop for JFK," I said in a voice that implored his help.

"Yeah lady, for tomorrow morning. You missed the last bus."

"Oh no! What am I going to do now?" I pleaded with even more urgency while looking back at my soon-to-be attacker.

I guess he noticed stark horror on my face. "Come on, get in. I've gotta turn this bus in near JFK anyway."

I jumped on that bus so fast. I didn't care where it was going.

Thanking the bus driver profusely, I hauled my bags up the steps and grabbed a seat. Then I looked out the window to see what had happened to my would-be assailant. A few feet away from the bus, he stood there, glaring up at me with stone-cold eyes. His source for his next fix had just escaped.

My heart was still pounding, and looking around I found myself alone again. I was the only person on this big bus late at night, except this time maybe I had a chance of getting to where I needed to go.

I'd never been on a bus from the city. So if we took off in the wrong direction, I wouldn't know the difference. I was thinking, "I hope the driver doesn't kill me – he seems so nice."

How much worse could it get? By now this stressful trek that had kept me up for close to twenty-four hours was taking its toll.

The next thing I knew, the bus driver was tapping me on the shoulder. "Hey lady, wake up."

I shot straight up in the air and screamed. I took a karate stance, which looked pretty ridiculous, since I didn't know karate. Totally out of it, I didn't know where I was or why I was on a bus, much less who this man was waking me up.

He backed away from me and pointed out the window. "Lady, we're here, JFK airport. You fell asleep."

As I got off the bus I thanked the driver wholeheartedly for being an angel. He'd saved my life.

SHOPPING ADVENTURES WITH NAOMI

Following every trip, I looked forward to going out for a long walk around the neighborhood to get some fresh air and detox my lungs. There's something about having been locked in a metal tube for three days that makes you want to be outside.

But today was even more special. I took a deep breath. *I'm in the sunshine and glad to be alive, especially after that commuting ordeal the night before.*

A couple of blocks into my walk, Naomi drove up beside me and stopped.

"Hey girl, get in. Let's go shopping. Filene's is having a sale."

I tried to explain that I needed to walk, but there was no arguing with Naomi. As far as she was concerned, I could get my oxygen and exercise while shopping. So I hopped in the car.

Looking down at my tennis shoes, shorts, and tee shirt, I said, "I'm not exactly dressed properly to go shopping in Manhasset's exclusive Miracle Mile."

She laughed but she wouldn't accept any excuse for me not to go. "Don't worry. You needed to get out anyway. I know your aunt has got you in there playing cards with her. She's addicted." She threw the car into gear. "Has she got you playing bridge with her group yet?"

"Oh no. Are you kidding? They would trump all over me. I'm just a beginner. Come to think of it I think that's where Willa is right now, out with her bridge club."

"Willa and I are both lucky that we're still able to drive – and shop," Naomi said with a grin.

"Good grief, I don't know about Willa's driving." I raised my eyebrows. "The last time I rode in a car with Aunt Willa, I vowed never to do it again. Her eyesight has gotten worse with the macular degeneration. You know her daughters have told her in no uncertain terms not to drive."

"Yeah, I know," Naomi, said, as she drove right through a red light. She saw me pull back in the seat with the 'Oh Shit' look on my face.

"It was still yellow. Or close enough." She flipped her wrist as though it was no big deal.

"Holy shit, with you and Willa on the road it's much safer for me to be in an airplane. Do you know how Willa can tell if the stop light has turned green?"

"No. How?"

"All the other cars behind her start honking."

Naomi laughed out loud. Me too, knowing New York drivers, and how they sit on their horns.

Naomi then got serious, thinking about the implications of what I said. "Good Lord. I knew her eyesight had deteriorated, but I didn't know it had gotten that bad. Willa says she only drives a couple of blocks to get her hair done and to her bridge game."

As we actually stopped at the next stoplight, Naomi peered over the top of her sunglasses with a steely gaze and threw an incredulous look at me. "You don't believe that for a minute, do you? I can't imagine her daughters believe that's all she drives, either."

"Naomi, you know I do what I can. In between trips I'm always running errands in all directions, but I can't keep her off the road. You can't tell her anything. It's bad enough having to deal with those kinds of people on an airplane. The other day Mohamad Ali was on board one of our flights. A flight attendant walked by and reminded him to buckle his seatbelt. Ali said, 'Superman don't need no seatbelt.' And she said, 'Superman don't need no plane.' He grinned and fastened his seatbelt."

"Willa's not quite that bad." Naomi said with a wink. "She'll let you know what she's thinking in a heartbeat. Stubborn as hell, but that spitfire is a whole lot of fun and we have lots of laughs together. Let's go to Filene's first and then hit Lord & Taylor."

"Did you hear about Willa's last doctor's appointment? Carolyn came up from South Carolina to take her. The doctor told Willa, 'I'm prescribing this medication, but it can *not* be taken with alcohol.'

Willa said, 'I don't drink any alcohol.'

Carolyn reminded her about her nightly glass of wine and Willa said it didn't count."

OK, now I understand why Willa didn't consider wine as an alcoholic beverage. Her interpretation allowed her to keep on drinking. We'd better watch our elder generation like a hawk because they'll change the rules in a second to suit their needs. The closer I get to that age, the more I agree with that concept.

Naomi finally dropped me off at the house. Willa thought I had gone out for a really, really long walk that day. And I didn't tell her any different.

BE CAREFUL- LUGGAGE CAN SHIFT DURING TAKEOFF AND LANDING

I was the official greeter at the front door of the plane, welcoming the passengers and answering any questions.

"Good morning, welcome aboard," I said with a big smile.

The noticeable twang in my voice gave away a hint of my Southern hospitality. A young Hispanic lady boarded, carrying a newborn.

"Wow! That baby is tiny. Was she born yesterday? She's got to be the smallest baby I've ever seen on an airplane."

I was making light of the situation but also concerned about the regulation that a mother and baby must be medically stable and fit to fly.

"No speck English."

The Latin woman, who appeared to be traveling alone, walked past, as I made a mental note of her seat number. I turned to Janice, the purser. Janice has the final say about any potential problems that may arise during the flight. And if the mother or baby has any medical complications at 35,000 feet, guess who has to handle it? Me. And I don't want any emergencies or anybody bleeding on my flight.

"How old does a baby have to be to fly? Is it a month or six weeks?"

"It used to be a month, but now it's just a week, probably because there are so many of these women who come to Miami, deliver the baby, then immediately fly back home toting their new U.S. citizen. Besides, if they need a doctor's excuse, I'm sure their doctor would give them one."

Carmen, the designated Spanish-speaking flight attendant, walked up to the front. I shared my apprehension with her.

"You gotta come with me to see this tiny infant. I thought it was a child's doll. Will you ask the lady how old her baby is?"

Being a new mother herself, she said, "I can't believe these women jump on an airplane so soon after childbirth. It's bad enough to subject your own body to the pressurization changes on the plane, but I would never bring a newborn on with all these people coughing and sneezing. I just can't imagine that, think of all the infections and diseases a baby, with no immune system, could catch."

"Seriously," I said, "I was told not to take my new puppy to a pet store for the first six weeks until he'd had all his shots.

"Come on, she's in 12C on the aisle."

I pointed to the lady's seat toward the front of coach. There sat the new mother but with no baby in sight. Just then a man popped open the overhead bin above her and that's when we spotted the baby wrapped in a bundle of pink blankets. The man lifted his two-ton carry-on bag to sling it on top of her. I was terrified. Carmen and I both screamed - in English and Spanish. I don't know what startled the man more, us screaming at him or when he realized there was a live baby in the overhead bin.

The new mother screamed too.

Carmen explained to the lady when a child is not occupying a seat it should be on her lap and that's why it's classified as a 'lap child.'

Everyone finally calmed down and we finished boarding the flight. It finally registered with her that the overhead bin wasn't the proper place to keep a baby. Not only could the baby girl have been squashed, but also, if we had taken off, this three or four-pound baby would've slid from one end to the other along with all those huge fifty pound bags. There's no way she could have survived.

WHAT HAVE YOU GOT IN THIS GARMENT BAG?

I thought I'd seen it all with the newborn baby in the overhead bin. Carmine and I couldn't wait to tell the other flight attendants about it.

But Bunny, a flight attendant I attended international training with at the flight academy, had an even better story. And I got her to tell it again.

Bunny said, "I was helping a Spanish-speaking man hang his heavy garment bag in the closet. We struggled with the bag, which was almost as big as me. I joked with him and asked in Spanish, 'What do you have in here? Your grandmother?' "

He replied in Spanglish, '*Sí*. She die. I take her home.'

Even though I'd heard the story before, it just got better every time, especially watching the stunned looks on the faces of the other crew members.

Bunny went on, "I couldn't believe it. I thought maybe I didn't hear him right." I stopped and looked the man straight in his eyes. 'Did you say your grandmother is in *this* bag?'

'*Si*. She die. I take her home.' It was as if he were talking about the weather.

"I told him, 'Not on this plane, you don't. Bringing a dead body on board is not only creepy... but also illegal.' The airport and airline security were both called, along with the police. They even called the FBI and probably the CIA and ICE (Immigration and Customs Enforcement) because it was an international flight."

Bunny added, "I think this would make a great Latin American version of the movie *National Lampoon's Vacation*. Remember, when Clark Griswold (Chevy Chase) transported his wife's dead Aunt Edna to Phoenix in a tarp secured on top of the station wagon?

Just like Clark Griswold, the passenger thought he'd found a way to transport his grandmother home...at no cost to him."

THE NEW M.H.C.
(MILE HIGH CLUB)
AND OTHER TALES

Aunt Willa and I met her buddies for lunch the day after I got back from one of my trips. Mary Ann, the diva of high fashion in the group, greeted me as I pulled up a chair.

"Elizabeth, how are you doing? Been on any good trips lately?"

I knew she was asking did I have any good stories. And I did.

"OK, actually something did happen on my flight last night. You've heard of the Mile High Club? Right?"

They all responded at once, "Ohhh yeah!"

Aunt Willa gave me that look. She had a way of cutting her eyes at me that I knew was a warning. The rest of the group eagerly sat forward, wide-eyed, and ready to listen to what I had to say.

"Well, I was working in first class on an A300 Airbus, which in layman's terms is a big-ass airplane. A newbie, wet-behind-the-ears flight attendant, Amanda, came running up to the front from coach totally discombobulated. She popped the cockpit door open, took a step inside, not waiting for the two pilots to respond. 'There's a couple in the lav in the back joining the Mile High Club.'

"The pilots looked at each other then back to the flight attendant. The first officer gave out a little snicker, and the captain tried to suppress his grin, but the crinkles in the corners of his eyes gave him away.

"'What am I supposed to do?' She looked at them all flustered. 'They're making all kinds of noises.'

"The captain assured her, 'Don't worry. It'll be over in a minute.' Then he added, 'But if it becomes a real problem, you let me know.'

"Not even two minutes later, Amanda blasted into the cockpit again. 'You won't believe this! There were three people in the lav.' She started karate chopping the air with her elbows to show the scale of difficulty in such a restricted space.

"The captain held up three fingers. 'Three...three people. You've got to be kidding me...how on earth?' "

The luncheon ladies all gasped. Naomi had been quiet for a full minute, which was unusual for that redhead.

She threw her head back, and said, "I think that should be classified as a new category of the M.H.C. They should be given a new elite customer reward status of Gold or Platinum...maybe even Diamond. This is definitely not the normal level of achievement. Think of the old timey telephone booth stuffing fad or the circus clown routine involving an implausibly large number of clowns emerging from a very small car. This beats them all."

"Elizabeth," Aunt Willa said to me, "not that you could beat that story, but tell them about Dolly Parton."

"Oh, yeah. She was on my flight last week. We hung what appeared to be her expensive coat in the closet in the front of the plane. You know, the one in between first class and the forward lav. Well, in the middle of the flight, Jeffrey, a flight attendant snuck up to the front and opened the closet door. When no one was looking, as inconspicuously as possible, he pulled the sleeve of her coat out then proceeded to caress it as if it were a Persian cat.

"He didn't notice when Dolly got up to go to the bathroom. She bumped right into him as she walked around the corner.

"She was more attractive in person than she appears on screen, friendly and good-natured, but even so I wondered how she would handle this situation.

"Jeffrey told me that Dolly looked surprised, but she didn't miss a beat, 'Honey, you can try that coat on. You help yourself, if you like that ole thing.' She started pulling it out of the closet. 'It is soft, isn't it?'

"Jeffrey not only tried it on, but then he sashayed up and down the aisle of the airplane. He did a few fashion runway pirouettes every now and then, to let everyone know he had on Dolly Parton's coat."

"Did the passengers say anything about it?" asked Ethel.

"Are you kidding? They loved it. Everybody had seen Dolly board the plane, so they knew the coat belonged to her. The impromptu fashion show entertained everyone!"

Since most of the ladies had taken multiple trips around the world, they were a lot more knowledgeable than me about interesting places and exotic travels. But Aunt Willa had the showstopper.

She said in a casual tone as she buttered a roll, "Buck and I went on a trip to Africa and stayed in a tree house."

"Wait, wait, wait, back it up. What did you say?" My aunt didn't own a pair of blue jeans, never did any outdoor activities that I knew of, so her staying in anything other than luxury accommodations would've been out of the question. I was picturing the typical tree house in the back yard, like the one I'd played in as a kid.

"We stayed in an African tree-house hotel, which has luxury suites built at canopy level, in giant baobab trees that are hundreds of years old."

My mind shot back to all the years she sat at the kitchen table working on the *New York Times* crossword puzzle every morning. It fascinated me that she could remember those facts and strange names. You could ask her the name of some bizarre mushroom that only grows in the rain forest of the Amazon, and she wouldn't hesitate to respond with the correct answer.

A part of me wanted to know why I couldn't have gotten that gene. I have trouble just remembering simple things. Like that joke my preacher told me I need to start thinking about the Hereafter and I told him I do all the time. I walk into a room and say to myself, "What am I... here after?"

Now I knew why Aunt Willa knew all the African trivia. At this point, she had everyone's attention.

"They have four-poster beds, a Jacuzzi, and most importantly, a toilet. After a long day on a safari, we would enjoy a drink on the private balcony with spectacular views of the forest. Then during the night and mostly during the early morning, the animals came to drink out of the watering hole right beneath us. We saw elephants, giraffes, and tons of other wildlife that we would never have seen so close anywhere else."

When she described it, I thought that sounded more like my Aunt Willa's style of vacation. I'd never heard of the African tree-house hotels. But being the animal lover that I am, this vacation has definitely been added to my bucket list. And she got everyone's mind off the Mile High Club.

HAZING THE NEW FLIGHT ATTENDANTS

At lunch with my Aunt Willa and her friends, they wanted to know more about my job in the skies.

Pat asked me, "What's it like to be locked on the airplane with all those people? I imagine some of the flight attendants can have an attitude, too."

I thought about it.

"I love my job, and I love talking to people, but you're right, some of the senior flight attendants can be really mean.

"On my first trip on a DC10 airplane, the purser asked me to go to the lower lobe galley for supplies. 'Okay, sure,' I said, as I got into the elevator located the middle of the galley. This elevator is the smallest elevator I'd ever seen, just wide enough to hold one person. Some of us call it a "stand-up coffin."

"I could never do that." Mary Ann said. "I have claustrophobia, and I'll have nightmares just thinking about it."

"Well, it gets worse. You are really going to love this part. The elevator started moving down with a slow rumble, then stopped in the middle of nowhere. Dead stop. No exit. No way of knowing what was happening. Stuck in this black hole, I immediately thought, 'Uh-oh. There's something wrong with the airplane.' In a panic, I turned a complete circle, searching at eye-level for the controls. I could hear laughter from above, so, looking up to see where it was coming from, I found the elevator switches in an out of the way place. The purser had pushed the master control button, which I knew nothing about, to stop the elevator.

Through a little window at the top they could watch me, the panic-stricken, claustrophobic junior flight attendant, trying desperately to figure out how to get out. The senior mamas loved to play this prank on all the newbies. Maybe they thought it was funny, but it scared the shit out of me."

"Did you try to get them back?" asked Mary Ann.

"There's not much I could do because I still had to work with these people. But to get even with the not so pleasant, prehistoric, senior mamas, we gave them nicknames, behind their backs, of course. There was: Diana-saurus Rex, Terry-Dactyl, and Anna-conda.

"Overall, most flight attendants, even the senior mamas, are nice to work with. But every duty on an airplane involves teamwork. New flight attendants have to learn the flow of the service—who does what, when, and how. And some of the flight attendants have different ways of giving input.

"It's just like every other job. Some people are nice; some are difficult."

I thought about it for a second. "The biggest difference is being locked in a confined space with people who are having a bad day. Sometimes it feels like you're in this pressure cooker for an eternity."

WHO LET THE DOGS OUT?

You know how it is when you get a bunch of good friends together. Sometimes it is a really, really long lunch.

As our chatter continued I told the ladies, not all the flight attendants that picked on us were mean. Some were just mischievous.

Recently, I'd worked on a huge A300 Airbus that held two hundred and fifty-two people in coach with dual aisles. While standing in the back galley during the flight, a dog barked. I knew that the cargo section, which held the animals, was located right underneath us so I didn't think much about it. Then the dog barked again.

I turned to José, the galley flight attendant. "Did you hear that dog bark?"

He said, very seriously, "Yes. If you bark, it'll bark back at you. He's lonely."

So I barked. "Woof, woof, woof."

Wouldn't you know it – the dog barked again. The louder I barked, the more the dog barked back. About this time, another crew member walked up, and I invited her to join in the excitement.

"Bark at that dog. He'll bark back at you. He's lonely." I pointed down to the area below us.

She barked at the dog, too. José prodded us on, and pretty soon there were six flight attendants barking in the back galley, on an airplane packed to the gills.

Sandra, the flight attendant who had worked the beverage cart with José, said, "I heard that dog all the way up the aisle."

We kept on barking, and sure enough that dog barked back each time. José had us barking up a storm. He reeled us in, hook, line and sinker.

This went on until José couldn't control himself any longer. He started laughing so hard that he could barely speak, and couldn't continue his charade.

When he finally stopped laughing, we figured out there was no dog. And we figured out that José was a talented ventriloquist.

BOARDING INTERNATIONAL FLIGHTS

My conversations with the luncheon ladies jogged up more memories of incidents that have happened throughout the years. Before 9/11, airline travel was much more casual and passengers brought on anything they could carry. The baggage sizer at the security checkpoint is what finally put an end to it.

I remember years ago while boarding flights to Haiti, we often found people sitting on top of huge Costco 24-packs of toilet paper or diapers or anything else that came packaged to serve an army. Of course, we would have to store these treasures somewhere, so the passenger could fit in their seat. Some ladies came in wearing four or five big hats, one on top of another. The hat decorated with the most ribbons, flowers, and feathers would typically be perched on the top of the pile. There's no regulation about hats but they certainly added to the entertainment during the boarding parade.

And then there was the time...

OKAY, WHAT ARE YOU DRAGGING IN THE BURLAP BAG?

I have witnessed everything inside an airplane from car bumpers, to furniture, to live animals including talking parrots that wouldn't shut up. Even snakes, which weren't supposed to be loose in the airplane.

Keep in mind that this was before 9/11, when there were far fewer restrictions on every phase of air travel. During boarding on a flight from Miami to Guatemala, a man was dragging an extra-long burlap bag on the floor behind him. It resembled one used for picking cotton, only this one contained lots of big bulges that looked like bowling balls. I could tell by his struggle to the back of the plane that this so called carry-on-bag weighed an enormous amount. I was prepared for him to ask me to help put his load in an overhead bin, but then my curiosity got the best of me.

I asked, "OK, let me guess? Are you going to a bowling tournament?"

"No," he said, "frozen turkeys."

To be exact, he had eight frozen turkeys. He was going home for Thanksgiving, and, according to him, the USA produced plumper turkeys.

Boarding can be a zoo!

WINDOW EXIT BRIEFING

Some passengers request the exit row because of the extra legroom. Some people think it's just another seat number in the middle of the plane and are oblivious to the exit row requirements.

Apparently, there have been emergency situations in which passengers didn't realize the funny looking over-sized window with 'Emergency Exit' written on it was indeed there for a purpose. They also didn't realize the responsibility for opening it rested with the people closest to it.

So now we have to ask each passenger in one of these seats, "Are you willing and able to open this exit in case of an emergency?"

Here's the kicker: since this requirement has been implemented, only one woman has ever asked me any questions about what would happen in an emergency situation. During the exit briefing, she pointed to the briefing card.

"How do you get off the wing down to the ground? According to this, it doesn't show any way to do that."

I looked at her, amazed.

"Did you know that you're the only person that has ever asked me any questions? Most people don't even read the briefing card. You're absolutely correct."

The woman smiled, pleased with herself. I continued talking loud enough for everyone around me to hear.

"Each airplane is different. The window exits on a 737 airplane are a last resort in an evacuation because the exit is over the wing. From the wing you will have to jump to the ground. All the other door exits have huge inflatable slides that deploy, which enable a quicker and easier exit."

This woman listened intently with her brow furrowed. "Am I the only person who has shown any interest in this?"

"You certainly are!" I nodded my head and smiled at her.

"Hmm. These exits are self-service. That means that a passenger who hasn't paid any attention to the safety information might just jump out of the window if anything happens."

"Yep. Except for the ones that don't even know there is an exit there."

"You mean like that one." Her gaze turned toward the teenage surfer dude at another window exit. He swayed to the music in his ear buds, totally obsessed with thumbing the video game on his iPhone.

"That's scary!"

I had to agree.

RUN FOR YOUR LIFE, IT'S SMOKE, IT'S FIRE...NO...IT'S CONDENSATION

If you have ever been to Miami, then you know about its high temperatures and the humidity that makes a person feel worse than being in a sauna.

Like my neighbor used to say, "It's so hot, my clothes are wringin' wet."

In such conditions a plane heats up while not in use on the ground. Then, right before boarding, the air conditioning is turned on full blast to cool the plane as quickly as possible. The combination of the cold airflow interacting with the high humidity condenses in the hot airplane, creating a layer of moisture as thick as smoke.

During boarding on one of these hot-steamy days, the passengers saw what they mistook for smoke coming out of the air-conditioner vents. The flight attendants made an announcement over the PA.

"Don't be alarmed. It's condensation."

But it was too late. Two of the passengers had already opened the window exit and were standing outside on the wing. We had to get them back inside the airplane while the aisle was packed with people trying to get to their seats.

Then, one of their impatient fellow passengers pointed to the open window exit and said to the evacuees, "Are you crazy? What're you doing? Who told you to evacuate? We're still sitting at the gate."

They said in their defense, "We thought we were supposed to open this exit or something, if there's a fire."

Another time, directly adjacent to the window exit, sat a white-haired lady dressed in a prim and proper outfit - a skirt with a matching jacket. I could picture her flying a while back in the early 1960s when passengers took pride in how they presented themselves and arrived at the airport in their Sunday best. The men wore suits and ties. The women wore Jackie Kennedy pillbox hats and white gloves, along with their fashionable dresses.

The elderly lady gave the flight attendant an amenable response that she understood and would be responsible for the window exit in case of an emergency. With no further questions from this passenger who was now studying the window exit, the flight attendant turned to leave. A loud *whoosh* sound caused her to turn around. There in front of her was a wide-open window exit.

Jumping out of his seat the lady's husband said, "What did you do?"

She shrugged her shoulders, and gave a sincere and innocent argument.

"Well, I just wanted to make sure I could open it."

The window closed again easily, but there were repercussions. It had to be inspected by a maintenance person who, as usual, took a long time to get to the plane. And then the required paperwork explaining the incident had to be completed, which resulted in a long delay.

One of the passengers, had a few stern remarks, "Who would've thought someone would do something like that? When some people check into the airport, they leave their brains at the curb."

SAFETY DEMO

While working one of her first flights, rookie F/A Karen unintentionally made sure a certain passenger had a good flight. As the airplane started to taxi out, Karen gathered up the demo equipment and, along with her fellow flight attendants, lined up in the aisle to perform a manual safety demonstration.

Karen brushed her thick, chestnut hair behind one ear and tidied her blouse and vest over her small uniform skirt for a last minute primp. She beamed a wide smile, as she stood in the front of the first class cabin in full view of all the passengers to perform the demo.

Everything proceeded as usual until unexpectedly the plane's brakes grabbed and slammed it to an abrupt halt. Karen lost her balance and catapulted into the arms of an accommodating businessman.

He wrapped his arms around her and boasted to the business associate seated next to him, "See? I told you this was going to be a good flight."

WHY YOU NEED TO BE IN YOUR SEAT

If you fly at all, you know the drill. The safety video is shown when the plane starts initial pushback. All of you must be in your seats when the FAA required manual or video safety demonstration is shown.

What passengers don't know is flight attendants have fun making bets on which passenger will invariably, at this time, decide to go to the bathroom or stand up to get something out of the overhead bin, thus blocking another passenger's view of the emergency procedures. On one flight, we had just begun to play the video when the man in 23C got up and headed for the bathroom.

I looked at Jack, the other F/A in charge of running the video equipment, "You won the bet this time, you lucky so and so. I should have known that fidgety man couldn't stay seated for long. You better stop the safety video until he gets out of the lav, and if he takes too long we have to call the captain to delay the taxi out."

"Why do these people think they can stand up while the plane is moving?"

Jack pushed the pause button on the video and then turned to me and the other flight attendant.

"If left up to the discretion of most passengers, they wouldn't care if we had FAA regulations at all, or at the very least had something similar to some of the European airlines."

"Holy cow, have y'all heard some of the stories about Aeroflot, the Russian carrier?" I asked my co-workers. "My friend Lynne flew on them. She said most of the seatbelts were dangling throughout the flight, that is, if you were lucky enough to even have a seatbelt. Also, if there were any safety regulations, they weren't enforced. Lynne and her husband once sat across the aisle from a family who, before takeoff, proceeded to pull down all their tray tables and set up a typical Indian meal. Then, because there was no warning to stow their opened containers and put up their tray tables for takeoff, all of their dishes slid off into their laps."

"Eww. Gross. What a mess," Jack said, as he pushed the button to continue the safety video when Mr. 23C returned to his seat.

"Yeah, Lynne told me that was twenty years ago when there were smoking flights but no one paid any attention to a 'smoking section' as such. The smokers walked up and down the aisles dropping ashes on everyone. The man right behind Lynne lit up a cigarette. The flight attendant just shrugged and wouldn't say anything to him."

The galley flight attendant said, "Oh man! I bet those were rough flights to work. The Russians have a reputation for drinking a lot of vodka, too."

"But it gets worse. Not only did none of the bathroom doors lock, but also on a flight from Moscow to St. Petersburg, people packed in like a rush-hour subway and stood in the aisle during the flight.

With no reservation system, the flight was overbooked so the passengers who didn't have seats had to stand for the entire flight."

"Good grief," said Jack. "Hey, I heard recently that Ryanair, the low-cost airline in Europe, tried to do the same thing. They tried to get approval to sell standing-room only tickets to pack in more people. Just think about the nightmare those flights would be. Only good thing is – no beverage or meal service because we wouldn't be able to get the cart through. And heaven forbid if someone had a heart attack on a flight like that."

This brought up reminiscences about some of my friends who have been severely injured while on duty.

"You know, a dozen or so flight attendants are disabled every year from breaking their necks, not to mention all the ruptured discs and broken bones, and that's just the ones I know about on our airline. At least the U.S. has these regulations in place to try to protect you, the passenger. Can you imagine how many more accidents would happen if passengers were flopping around during the flight?"

WHAT LIFE VEST?
AND DON'T TAKE ANYTHING WITH YOU!

The safety information provided on an airplane comes into play only in an emergency situation. Most people ignore it. They don't think anything could ever happen to them.

The evacuation of a plane on the Hudson River demonstrated the consequences of this devil-may-care attitude. On January 15, 2009, US Airways Flight 1549, from LaGuardia to Charlotte, N.C., ditched into the frigid river because the plane hit a flock of geese. Many of the passengers stood on the wing, waiting to be rescued, with no life vests on.

REeeaaLLY! Come on now.

If you had just crash-landed into freezing water and survived so far, wouldn't you think to grab either the seat cushion as a floatation device or the life vest underneath the seat?

These passengers were pushing their luck after Captain Sullenberger, along with the first officer, Jeffrey B. Skiles, did a miraculous job of saving their lives. The two were highly commended because it takes the coordination of both pilots to handle an emergency situation. The flight attendants also did a heroic job, considering their unprecedented situation. I can't imagine what went through their minds when the emergency evacuation came to a screeching halt. The first people out the window exits stopped on the crowded wings with nowhere to go until the rescue boats arrived. The flight attendants along with the remaining passengers were trapped inside the plane as the freezing water rushed in.

High five to all the crew members for handling such a horrendous ordeal so skillfully.

Another evacuation happened recently in Las Vegas, and the news showed some of the passengers getting off the emergency slide with their luggage, duty-free, and souvenirs. They endangered the lives of the other passengers and crew, not to mention the volunteer helpers and emergency personnel at the bottom of the slide who dodged the heavy luggage flying at them. My friend, Doris, says that F/As don't vent we "share" stories. So I "shared" what I knew about the incident with my cousin Carl.

"I hope those people got reprimanded for taking things with them. Don't they think of it as a life or death situation? Don't they know that every second counts for the people still on the plane behind them, while they're taking valuable time retrieving their luggage full of souvenirs and underwear?

"I've seen a passenger who survived a plane crash. They brought him on in a wheelchair and sat him right in front of my jump seat. I gave him a million blankets after he explained that this was his first flight since the accident. As one of the few people to live through the ordeal he has no temperature control due to burns over sixty percent of his body. I did anything possible to keep him comfortable because I couldn't imagine how he coped with the stress of being on this flight. I tried not to think about what happened to him but his presence couldn't be ignored when he was so close. I'll never forget him and the look in his eyes."

Carl said, "I'd just like to see someone try and open an overhead bin if that person is between me and the exit of an airplane that's on fire. I can't imagine what I would do but it's just so hard to believe that people are that callous and heartless when others' lives are in danger."

"I agree. I also heard the Hudson River crash passengers did the same thing, grabbed their luggage. Those people were in for a rude awakening when the rescue boats showed up. They were told that the boats were for people only and to drop their luggage in the river right then and there. The people who had followed the instructions not to take anything with them got their luggage back in a few months."

LOST IN TRANSLATION: WHAT DID HE JUST SAY? NO, HE DIDN'T!

With regard to safety procedures on an airplane, most passengers don't seem to listen to the safety announcements – unless, of course, there's a *faux pas*.

These days everyone is accustomed to non-smoking flights, but when I first started working, smoking was permitted. The last few rows on the plane were designated as a smoking area. Oftentimes no one wanted to sit in this section or anywhere close to it, even the smokers. No one fancied being forced to breathe fumes for hours and have their hair and clothes reek of tobacco smoke when they deplaned.

Serious confrontations and even fights between the smokers and non-smokers became inevitable during the difficult boarding process while seating passengers.

Once in the air, people were allowed to stand in the back of the plane to smoke, so we frequently called the pilots to turn on the *No Smoking Sign* due to smoke so thick that we couldn't see our hands in front of our faces. I know that's a cliché but I mean it quite literally.

I can't recall any bar I've ever been in having worse air quality than the recycled air on those smoking flights.

All flights before 1998 allowed smoking on board. So the safety regulations had to be geared to the fire hazards of smoking. One section of the safety announcement stated: 'Smoking in the lavatory or tampering with, disabling, or destroying smoke detectors could result in a fine.' Back in those days there was another statement in the safety announcement that cigar and pipe smoking were not allowed in the lav or while standing in the aisle.

One of the flights I worked from New York to Montreal, Canada, not only was a smoking flight, but also a destination that required the safety demo in both English and French. Our French-speaking male flight attendant, Ivan, read the information as we performed the manual safety demonstration. He got tongue-tied right in the middle and just stopped...dead silence. That left the rest of us flight attendants lined up in the aisle, facing the passengers, oblivious to what had transpired, and with nothing to do without our announcer.

Standing in the middle of the aisle in coach, I felt all eyes upon me. I just wanted to hurry up and end this tortuous demo because I didn't understand a word of French. I just knew the sequence of what I was supposed to do, which included showing how to use a seat belt, an oxygen mask and holding up a safety-briefing card.

During this long pause everyone started laughing, including Ivan.

The thought occurred to me that maybe it was something I'd done. *Oh Lordy, do I have a rip in the seat of my pants? Is my zipper down? Do I have toilet paper stuck to the bottom of my shoe?* I couldn't figure it out, but the French-speaking passengers started whispering among themselves. That was my first clue. Then Ivan broke out in uncontrollable laughter again.

Well, it turned out that in French, the word for pipe smoking and the word for what Monica Lewinsky did with President Clinton (when he swore he did not have sex with that woman) were very similar.

While reading the safety instructions, Ivan had inadvertently told the passengers no one was allowed to do a 'Bill Clinton' in the lav or while standing in the aisle! When he realized what he'd said, he started laughing and couldn't stop. It took him what felt like forever to regain his composure enough to finish the announcements. I still see him every once in a while and give him a hard time about his *faux pas*.

"Hey Ivan, you been smoking any pipes in the aisle lately?"

TAXI OUT

I think we're finally ready for takeoff. The passengers are settled in their seats, seat belts fastened. Your flight attendant, that would be me, is in the jump seat and taking a deep breath after accomplishing the worst part of the flight – boarding. What else could possibly happen?

CHILD'S TIME OUT

On this flight, I fastened my seatbelt into the aisle side of the double-jump seat next to Sharon, the purser, in the front of the plane. As we taxied out onto the tarmac to prepare for takeoff, I glanced down the aisle for the final security check. What I saw made me shake my head.

"Sharon. Don't be alarmed."

She saw the surprised look on my face, because I wasn't expecting to see someone running up the aisle toward me.

"What is it? What's wrong?"

The closet wall was right in front of Sharon, obscuring her view, so she unsnapped her seatbelt and leaned over in my direction, anxiously trying to see down the aisle.

Sharon and I both watched a little boy, about four years old, with his arms and legs pumping as he ran full force up the aisle in our direction. He sported a striped tee shirt, shorts, and what looked like strobe lights on his sneakers. His mother sprinted close behind him. All the passengers looked up as they heard the thumping of his steps and saw something short swish by their seats followed by a lady running to try to catch it. His mother finally caught up with him just as he dashed into the corner of the galley beside us.

"I told him if he didn't behave he would have to go to time-out and I think he took me literally," his mother apologized. "He took off running. I guess this was the only corner he could find to do his time-out penance."

Children have given us precious few problems relative to the other passengers we've had to deal with on a daily basis. I just wish a time-out strategy could be implemented with misbehaving, unruly adults as well.

Elizabeth Calwell

DEPORTEES, HANDCUFFS, SHACKLES and CHAINS

A deportee is a person who, for whatever reason, is being expelled from a country. It could be for a criminal offense, illegal entry into the country, or simply because the person lost a passport and could not enter or remain in the country.

Sometimes having a deportee on board presents special problems. On one of my first trips on a 727 jet, I worked in coach with Jane, a senior mama. As we prepared for the flight, Jane hustled around, setting up the galley in near record time. The cleaners and ground crew scurried in and out the back door from the lowered stairs (airstair) in the back of the plane. I just tried to stay out of everybody's way until boarding started.

The Boeing 727, a mid-sized narrow body jet, has since been retired. A unique feature of this airplane was the built-in airstair that opened from the rear underbelly of the fuselage and extended down to the tarmac, similar to pull-down attic stairs in a house.

In early versions of this aircraft, this door could be opened in mid-flight, but after a few surprising incidents, Boeing re-engineered it. They added a mechanical wedge, called the Cooper Vane, which prevented deploying the stair in flight. It was named after the infamous D.B. Cooper, who, after hijacking a 727, opened the airstair and parachuted somewhere over the Pacific Northwest with $200,000 in ransom money in his backpack. Never to be seen again.

As soon as our plane was ready for this particular flight, a deportee escorted by the authorities pre-boarded from the front entrance, ahead of the other passengers. The policemen seated him in the last row with no explanation and then retreated to the jet bridge, guarding the forward entrance of the plane until departure. That's all they were required to do in this case - make sure he got settled on the plane and that he didn't run out the front door.

On seeing this, Jane grabbed the phone and yelled over the PA to the flight attendants in the front, "Get those police back on this plane. It's not my job to guard a deportee."

She calmly continued stocking the beverage cart, and then turned to me, waving a handful of napkins.

"I'm not babysitting any more deportees. Just last month, they did the same thing. The deportee simply got up and walked out the back door, down the stairs to freedom."

Even though this deportee appeared fairly easy-going and unassuming, the officers came back on and stayed with him, until the stairs were retracted and the rear door was closed and latched. With everything secured, the two guards started to make their way back to their station at the front door of the plane.

As they passed by Jane, she said, "I suppose if this guy made a break for it, I could trip him. But believe it or not, it's one of the very few things that's not in my job description."

On another flight, while working first class, we ran out of Bloody Mary mix, so I proceeded toward the back galley for more supplies. The line of people to use the bathroom blocked the way, and I stopped short, next to a row of three male passengers. The man in the middle flashed me a big grin; I smiled back at him. He started flirting with me, raising his voice in a booming announcement to everyone around him.

"You're sooo beautiful. Where have you been hiding during this flight? I want you to stay back here!"

My eyebrows went sky high. I scanned the men on either side of him for an explanation for his outrageous behavior. My eyes darted ahead of the crowd, searching for the other two flight attendants. *Why was this man shouting at me?* Both of them broke out laughing when they saw the face I made as I scrutinized the passenger. The two men next to him were laughing too. I knew something was up but couldn't quite grasp the full picture. The flight attendant standing in the back galley gave me a hand signal that I should look at the flirting passenger's wrist. I looked down and saw that he was attempting to hide the handcuffs shackling his wrists under the tray table. I couldn't believe it.

The flirtatious prisoner continued bestowing creative compliments on every female heading toward the bathroom.

As I turned to walk back to first class I overheard him tell a rather plus-sized woman, "Oh honey, I really looove a big woman, for shade in the summer, warmth in the winter and traction in the snow."

He said it with such charm that she just laughed, right along with everyone else.

I don't know why this man was in police custody. It had to have been something serious for him to warrant two escorts and be confined with handcuffs, but it didn't slow him down one bit.

On another flight, my friend Karin told me of her encounter with a deportee. Karin and her crew were doing an Orlando turn (going to Orlando, turn around and then back to Miami). This was their second leg of the day, so during the down time between flights, they got off the plane to get something to eat. As they walked through the gate area, which was full of passengers for multiple flights, the crew passed by a man they presumed was a deportee, sitting between two police officers who appeared to be I.N.S. agents (Immigration and Naturalization Service).

Thinking nothing of it, the crew returned and began to board the flight as usual.

A few minutes later, one of the flight attendants noticed a male passenger going into the aft lav and when he came out he had changed into different clothes. Since this was pre-9/11, she dismissed the quick-change artist. People change clothes all the time because they're hot or cold. It's just no big deal. The male passenger then hurried out of the bathroom, and headed at a fast pace up the aisle toward his seat.

Karin's co-worker, thinking the man had returned to his seat, sat down in her jump seat to prepare for takeoff in the rear of the plane. Karin hadn't seen any of this because she'd been setting up the aft galley during boarding.

The plane started moving. The wing walkers, the ground personnel who walk under the tips of the wings during arrival and pushback of the plane, began escorting the plane as it taxied out.

They coordinate with the lead marshal/wing walker by holding up orange-colored wands as a communication tool. These ramp workers watch for hazards and ensure the wing tip clearance of a $75,000,000 wide-body aircraft when parked in a confined area.

The airplane started moving forward.

As the plane taxied out, the flight attendants heard an outburst in the middle of the cabin. Karin lept out of her jump seat to see unexplained bright sunshine lighting up a broad swath of the middle of the cabin. As she got closer she realized the emergency window exit was open.

She ran up to the three people sitting in that row with their seatbelts still fastened and yelled, "What happened? Who did this?"

The passengers all pointed out the opening, but with the ruckus going on and everyone talking at once, Karin didn't understand. She thought perhaps something had malfunctioned in the window, so she crawled over the passengers and looked out the open exit. The plane was still moving. The wing walkers on the ground attempted to communicate with her by using their wands to point at something; but from her awkward angle over the wing she couldn't see anything.

Karin ducked back into the plane, continuing to look for some explanation from all the people packing the aisle in both directions. The curiosity seekers, along with those who wanted to help, swarmed out of their seats. Screaming passengers surrounded her, and continued pointing to the open window exit. The confusion escalated as the upheaval got louder and louder. It seemed to Karin that everyone was placing the responsibility for this turmoil on her.

She kept repeating, "What? What happened?"

A frustrated man the size of a NFL player still seated in the exit row grabbed Karin by her lapels with both fists, got right in her face, and shouted, "The man sitting with the two police officers before the flight went out the window."

"Oh shit." Karin realized it was the deportee who had escaped.

She attempted to calm the distraught passengers when a frantic voice shouted from the back of the plane, "The man who jumped left a bomb in the bathroom."

He had seen that the man had changed clothes in the lav, run up the aisle, and jumped out the window.

Now everyone started screaming in panic.

All they heard was 'bomb,' which ricocheted up the aisle as the terrifying word was repeated. With the passengers already on the verge of chaos, this sent them over the top. Everyone jumped up at once, and grabbed their belongings to get off the plane. Karin tried to sound reassuring.

"Stay seated. There is no bomb." But the airplane was now in complete uproar. "He was a deportee," Karin screamed at the top of her lungs but she couldn't be heard over the pandemonium.

Four pilots in uniform who were on board commuting to work grabbed the emergency megaphones and told everyone to calm down and be seated.

All this transpired in a matter of seconds that felt much longer.

Meanwhile, out on the tarmac, the wing walkers, who had never encountered anything like this before, were stunned, but at last gave the signal for the captain to stop the plane.

The deportee led the airline ground workers on a merry chase across the tarmac, but they caught and tackled him to the ground. I guess he was a D.B Cooper wannabe. He just hadn't thought through his escape plan very well.

So remember, from now on, when you request the exit row for more legroom you might get more than you bargained for!

TELEVANGELISTS IN THE AIR

Another one of my 727 adventures happened on a flight returning to the U.S. from the Caribbean. After we finished the beverage service in coach I pulled down the retractable double jump seat between the two aft lavs and sat down for a short break. If I wanted to sit down I didn't have any other choice except this uncomfortable seat but it came with its own caveats. Whoever sat here had to switch from one side to the other to allow for the lav doors to open for people to go in, in other words, not much of a break.

As I enjoyed my moment of respite, a male passenger approached.

I didn't pay much attention until he stopped in front of me and said, "The last time I was on an airplane I was in shackles and chains."

Was I confused? Did I hear that right? I looked up to see a nicely dressed middle-aged gentleman in a suit and tie. With the loud engines on each side, flushing lavs, and people talking, maybe I'd misunderstood. I just couldn't imagine someone would offer that information to a perfect stranger.

"Pardon me. What did you say?"

He repeated it with a very matter of fact attitude.

"The last time I was on an airplane, I was in shackles and chains."

"OK, I'll bite. Why was that?"

He leaned an arm against the wall close to me, in an overly friendly manner. A big gold wristwatch winked at me.

"I went to prison because of the misguided activities of a certain Evangelical group."

Then I knew exactly who he was, especially with so many of the televangelists from the Carolinas under public scrutiny, but I didn't let on.

He went on as if we were talking about the weather. "Did my time and now I'm out."

"I see," I said, still not quite sure what to make of him. "Were you vacationing in the Caribbean?"

"Actually, I'm setting up a new church."

"With all the poverty in the Caribbean, you're...what?" I stopped short before I said something I shouldn't.

He proceeded to tell me some more details about the venture, but all I could do was stare at the big gold watch and think, he's fooled a whole new group of unsuspecting, innocent people into giving him money for what they think is a good cause. Here I've been hauling plastic garbage bags of clothes to give to the poor people in some of the countries I go to and he's hauling out any loot that he can squeeze out of them. His popularity in the U.S. had emerged about the same time as another popular Christian televangelist group, the PTL Club, which included a television show, theme park and real estate holdings. No one knows for sure what PTL meant, maybe Praise The Lord, or People That Love but in some circles it stood for *Pass the Loot*.

His companion, a much younger bleached-blonde, strutted on back to use the bathroom. She was poured into a tight, spandex dress and dripping in expensive jewelry. She fit right into the picture. I just couldn't believe he was so brazen about his lifestyle.

After this trip, I headed toward crew operations in the airport. A small boy, maybe eight years old, surprised me by following close behind right into the authorized personnel-only elevator. Then I realized he was in the care of another flight attendant. It turned out he was being escorted as part of the Airline Ambassador International organization. He had won the lottery of a lifetime to be chosen to come to the United States for life-changing medical treatment.

This child caught me off guard as I tried not to stare at his severely burned face and the nub that he had for a right hand. I attempted to cheer him up and make him feel welcome.

"Hey buddy, did you fly on a big airplane? Was it fun?" I said in my broken Spanglish, which he understood, and he reacted like any other small child getting personal attention. He smiled.

He could still manage to smile. The misshapen grin on his small face was enormous for someone who had been through so much.

This reminded me that there are good people and organizations in this world, to counter-balance the other ones.

When I got on the elevator, I was still disgusted with the sleazy televangelist from my flight, but my anger melted away to sadness when I saw the little boy, and then to joy when the child smiled.

AFTER TAKEOFF

Everybody loves Ruth. You're going to love Ruth, too. A thin, attractive blonde, she keeps everyone laughing with her infinite stash of jokes and stories. Ruth has a few years on me, although you wouldn't know it because she has ten times more energy. She's one of those colorful personalities who can remember every joke she's ever heard.

And when she retells it, she gets into the theatrics of the character, whether it's a country bumpkin getting on a bus or the voice of Ollie, the Norwegian farmer, "Vell, I'lla tell you vat happened dere."

The four coach flight attendants, including myself, were in the aft galley preparing for the meal service when Dawn, a tinier-than-petite female, came to the back from first class.

"Sorry guys, but I just had to come back for a second to take a breather."

"Why? What happened?" Ruth asked, as we gathered around.

"I'd just loaded up a tray of beverages to deliver in first class…"

"Uh-oh!" Ruth rolled her eyes.

"Well, it wasn't that bad. You know that linebacker-sized man in 3B?" Dawn did a muscle man crunch with her arms to emphasize how big he was. "Well, he tried to help me by reaching for his cocktail. His hand tipped the tray and a glass of water spilled on his T-shirt and blue jeans."

"Been there, done that, only I did the whole tray of drinks," said Sandy, the galley flight attendant.

Dawn went on with her venting, if you could call it that with her sweet little voice. "I apologized and gave him extra napkins. He didn't seem too upset about it, but his wife—you know the 'possum lady' with the narrow, little eyes, and the snout-like face? Well, she went ballistic, and barked at me, 'Don't you have another shirt?'"

"Another shirt? You gotta be kidding me?" Sandy shook her head, as the rest of us laughed, eyes wide in disbelief.

Dawn shrugged. "I hesitated for a second, looking into her beady eyes…just to make sure this woman was serious. Then I replied, 'Yes, I do. But frankly, I don't think it would fit him.'"

As we all had a good chuckle, Ruth said, "I'm glad it wasn't tomato juice or red wine. That lady would've had a heart attack."

"You're right." Dawn took a deep breath before she turned to head back up to first. "Thanks guys. I'd better get back up there."

I pulled my apron on, and as I tied it in the back, I asked the other girls, "Hey, do y'all mind if Ruth and I work together on the meal cart? Ruth and I were in initial training together." They all knew that meant that we had a special bond, like being in a foxhole together, but also Ruth and I had been steadfast friends ever since boot camp at the Charm Farm.

"Sure, no problem."

"What are the entrées today?"

"Beef or chicken. Surprise, surprise," Sandy said, as she finished loading up the entrée racks in the carts.

Ruth whispered to me, "Watch out. Those two on the beverage cart are bent on getting this service over with as quickly as possible."

"Shoot! Ruth, I hate having to go like a bat out of hell. I feel like we're just slinging the trays at people. And besides that, handling the hot entrees in a rush makes my face turn red and everyone thinks I'm having a hot flash."

Ruth handed me some extra napkins. "I know, but we'll trade and do the beverage cart on the next leg."

We started out in this competition not only to get the passengers served as quickly as possible, but also to stay ahead of the beverage cart blitzkrieg, with the two flight attendants who stayed right on our heels. Ruth and I hustled as fast as we could go. As we approached each new row, we repeated in rapid succession, "Beef? Or chicken? Beef or chicken? Beeforchicken?"

I moved the cart forward to the next row and a man declared in a booming voice, "I think I'll have some of that thar' beaver-chicken."

Well, that totally caught me off guard. I did a double take and looked at him to make sure he was serious. "Excuse me."

"Yeah. Beaver-chicken."

While trying to keep a straight face, I served him the chicken with no explanation. After all, doesn't everything taste like chicken?

Can you imagine when he settled in back at home and told his wife that he wanted her to cook some of that good old 'beaver-chicken' for dinner?

Ruth and I kept on making tracks with the meal service and working our way closer to the back of the plane. By this time, we had run out of chicken. I asked a male passenger, "Would you care for the beef for dinner?"

He glared fiercely, and demanded, with a Spanish accent, "I require chicken."

I said, "I'm so sorry, but we don't have any more chicken, all we have is beef. *No mas pollo.*"

He got even more defensive. "I require chicken. My ticket says that I require chicken."

His insistent ultimatum got Ruth's attention and she became involved in the conversation. We spoke in unison, "Show me your ticket."

Sure enough, he pulled out his boarding pass and pointed to where it was printed, **CHECK IN REQUIRED.**

He agreed to have the beef for dinner since we were out of 'Check In.'

Ruth never lets anything humorous slide by her. She couldn't wait until all the coach flight attendants gathered in the back galley. Even the people seated in the back row enjoyed the entertainment, as they heard Ruth's infectious laughter when she described the 'new menu item' just invented on this flight - beaver-chicken.

It's always fun to fly with Ruth. Her mantra is 'Laughter is the jewelry of life. To be able to laugh adds that special bling to your day.'

"Hey Ruth, tell them about that special passenger on your flight last week, when the same thing happened with the entrées."

Ruth didn't need much prompting from me to tell another story.

"Oh, that was a good one! It was another flight like this one. We ran out of beef. A male passenger said in a very huffy, matter-of-fact manner, 'I want the beef. I don't want that other one.' "

Ruth went on with the story, using her hand gestures for emphasis. "'OK, hold on a second. I'll double-check with the galley flight attendant to make sure there's not another beef somewhere.' When I returned to the man, I told him, 'No, I'm so sorry, but we don't have any more beef. Would you care for the pasta for dinner?'

The indignant man yelled out, 'I don't want shit.'

Ruth shook her head. 'Well, thank goodness, because we don't have any of *that* either.' "

It doesn't take much to get flight attendants talking. Since we were already in the process of chowing down quickly in the back galley, these food episodes set us on the road to reminiscing about other incidents that had happened on our flights.

Ruth had that mischievous twinkle in her eyes that she gets when she's on a roll, telling jokes or stories. "Hey y'all, on my last trip, I was right in the middle of handing out the hot towels in first class when the captain called back to us with the warning that we only had a short period of time to do the service before we would run into some turbulence. I started hurrying as fast as I could go, knowing we would have to sit down soon. The tray of hot towels was in my left hand, and I was using the tongs with my right hand.

"In my haste I accidentally dropped the little rolled up towel right in the dead center of a businessman's lap. Without thinking twice I dove after it - with the tongs. You should have seen the look of horror on his face! Seeing those metal tongs coming after his private parts, he immediately covered his jewels with both hands."

Ruth embellished her story by mimicking the poor man's panic.

"Can you imagine what was going through his mind?" I said. "He almost got circumcised on an airplane. Or else he could have arrived at his destination with his voice an octave higher."

"Ruth, what did you do about the towel?" another crew member asked.

"Ah, I let him keep it, but he was afraid of me the rest of the flight."

PASSENGERS WITH FUR AND FEATHERS

On my next trip, I worked in coach with Charles, the galley flight attendant. Even though he was fairly senior, you wouldn't have known it by looking at him. He was slim and fit, with thick brown hair. Charles had an easy-going personality and, as he set up the galley, we started talking.

He shared a story about the good old days when airlines served food on just about every flight, even the super-short ones. The first flights added meals to keep people occupied because there was no other means of entertainment available. The general public came to expect it and loved to complain about the quality and/or quantity of the food at 35,000 feet. Now, of course, the passengers really have something to complain about because the airlines have cut back on this expensive perk and there is no food on most flights.

"All of the food trays were individually hand-run from the galley in the back of the plane by the flight attendants," said Charles. "Sometimes there wasn't enough time to complete the service, much less clean it up before the plane landed. On one of those trips as the galley flight attendant, I managed getting everything set up easily, but keeping the meal service going on a 727, single-aisle airplane, from that tiny galley in the back proved to be *Mission Impossible.*"

His job was to stay in the galley, setting up the hundred and thirty-some trays for the other coach flight attendants to run out (in flight attendant-speak).

"Hey Charles, it was a single aisle, right?" one of the flight attendants said. "I flew on that airplane a long time ago, and I couldn't believe the back galley was the size of a thumbtack."

"Yeah, that's it alright," Charles replied and then described the galley area for us. "A 727 aircraft was configured with two passenger seats directly across the aisle from the galley. Seated there were two men who watched my every move. After takeoff, we immediately started the high-speed food service on the totally full flight. I started slinging entrees on the trays and handing them to the other two flight attendants as fast as possible. In the rush, one plate of food accidentally slipped out of my hand. It dropped in a pile on the floor, but with no time to stop the process, the big plateful of rice and mystery meat, I mean meatloaf, stayed right where it landed."

"Eww, what a mess," I said.

"It felt like Lucy in the chocolate factory scene, on the *I Love Lucy* show, when everything on the conveyor belt went by too fast to keep up with the pace. I was too preoccupied keeping the flight attendants running to pay attention to what happened next.

"I heard this strange noise." He held his enclosed fist up to his mouth like a duck-call. "Coo-coo-coo, and glanced down to see two pigeons on the floor, busy feasting on the rice. They'd appeared out of nowhere."

"I'll bet that stopped you in your tracks," I said.

"Yeah, it flustered me so bad that I yelled, 'Where the hell did these pigeons come from?'

98

"I glanced at the man seated next to the galley; he dropped his chin and shrugged his shoulders. Apparently, they'd been hidden in his carry-on bag. He felt it was such a shame to waste a perfectly good pigeon meal; he'd released his pets to eat the rice. Can you believe that?"

And I thought I pack too much stuff, but he definitely has me beat.

A man carrying carrier pigeons in his carry-on bag. Say that three times—real fast.

Charles' pigeon story started us on a roll of storytelling, so I shared one. A couple of months ago, a typical family of four boarded the plane. The son, who was probably around eight years old, led the way, followed by his mother, father, and sister. The boy carried a small box on board undercover to his seat in coach. No one thought anything about it.

A short time after takeoff, we had just gotten out of our jump seats to prepare for the beverage service when passengers on the left side in the back of the plane screamed and stood up, first one row, then the next row, and so on. As the activity continued on up the aisle, it looked like an orchestrated 'wave' at a football game.

In between the women screaming, all we heard was "Eeek" and "What is it?"

That's when the boy's mother came up to us and said, "I'm so sorry, but my son has accidentally released four of his pet mice." We three flight attendants just looked at her with an expression of...what did she expect us to do about it?

"We told him not to let them loose."

"Live mice?" We all looked at each other.

"Yes, I'm afraid so, four of them. I told him not to play with the mice and under no circumstances to open the box."

"Boys will be boys," my crew member said, half-joking.

From her perch on top of an empty seat, another female flight attendant said, "Oh, so that's what's terrorizing our airplane. Thank god it's just a kid's pet mice and not some other creature from the depths of my imagination."

We were relieved, or kind-of relieved anyway, but still had to figure out how to handle the situation. "How do we catch these varmints?" I said, as if I had any intention of trying.

Our purser made an announcement over the PA. "The four-legged marauders are not rats, but a boy's harmless pet mice. Please remain calm. We'll try to round them up as soon as possible."

"Famous last words! I don't see her back here trying to catch 'em," I said, looking up at my co-worker, who obviously had no intention of coming down off the seat for anything.

No one was happy about having rodents running around, even if they were pets. We had reports of those mice all over the plane, because every time one person's foot moved, someone would scream, thinking it was a mouse. Everyone was on mouse patrol, looking for those critters. Nobody slept on that wild ride.

The mice were the only ones having a fun ride. They probably had some really good snacks in the passengers' bags, and then went home with them as stowaways.

⮑   ᧞

Sometimes a flight attendant helps the gate agents check the tickets of passengers as they get on the flight. In airline lingo we call it plucking tickets. I helped the agents on a full flight from JFK to Dingo (Santo Domingo, Dominican Republic). After we'd processed the last passenger, the agent and I proceeded down the jet bridge together. I walked onto the plane then turned around to say goodbye to the agent who was preparing to shut the door. All of a sudden, we heard a loud and unusual sound above the noise of all the people trying to settle into their seats.

"Baaaaaa, baaaaaaa, baaaaaaa."

"I raised my eyebrows at the agent at the same time as she looked at me for an answer.

"What was that?"

Well, someone had snuck a goat onto the plane. It was in the lav next to the entrance door. Not a little goat, this was a good-sized future dinner. The agent made an announcement over the PA, in English and Spanish; if anyone had lost their goat, they needed to come forward to claim it. Everyone on the plane started laughing, probably wondering if they'd understood the announcement correctly. No one came to claim the illegal passenger.

The agent asked me, "How could they have gotten a goat on the plane?"

"Hey, I was right there with you checking tickets, and I didn't see anything except the usual chaos during boarding." Back then there was no security checkpoint like there is today, and every Dingo passenger had ten to twenty family members present in the gate area to send them off on his or her trip. Chaos doesn't even begin to describe the turmoil caused by these groups of mostly non-English speaking people, all trying to talk above each other and hug their many loved ones at the last minute.

The only explanation I could come up with was that a passenger must have smuggled the goat in a large duffle bag. People used to bring on bags plenty big enough to accommodate a large animal. But you'd think someone would've noticed the bag moving around and making strange noises. Maybe someone put a hat, raincoat, and sunglasses on the goat and walked it right through the middle of the crowd.

You'd think somebody would've noticed a weird passenger that looked like an old goat. But then again, it was New York.

ANIMAL MAGNETISM

Back in the good ole days, boarding a Santo Domingo flight out of New York was a notorious challenge for everyone because, from the ticket counter to the gate agents, everyone just passed the people right through, especially the boisterous and rowdy ones. There was, and still is, a common practice of pushing the problem passengers on through the system for the flight attendants to handle. And that's why we refer to this as "Push to Crew."

Obviously, I'm not talking about all the passengers.

Dominican passengers have a notorious reputation for drinking heavily on flights. Out of New York we would regularly have to confiscate their gallon bottles of *wicky,* (*wicky* is Spanglish for whiskey). Yes, *gallon* bottles of whiskey. They ignored the rule that the only alcohol to be consumed on board must be purchased from a flight attendant, so the amount someone downs could be monitored. On these pre-9/11 flights, people could bring as much liquid in their carry-on bags as they could handle. The purchases of alcohol from the duty free store, delivered to the plane, also fell under "the Don't Partake on Board Rule" but that didn't slow down those determined patrons.

Upon arrival in Santo Domingo (or anywhere), the flight attendants are required to wait until all passengers have deplaned before we're allowed to leave. As the last off, walking down the aisle, we would find numerous empty, gallon bottles on the floor, not even hidden under the seats. *Good gosh, it's only a three-hour flight!*

Most of the time we could figure out when someone was sneaking drinks using their own booze but often they kept a low profile. That is until they got drunk. By that time it was too late. That's when they got fired-up and full of revelry. These Santo Domingo flights always kept us on the lookout for something to happen.

Even after 9/11, some wacky people still slipped through the cracks and made it onto the plane.

The clock was ticking down on the last few minutes of boarding another Santo Domingo flight. So far this morning everything had gone smoothly until one of the flight attendants, Xhandra, noticed a purse sitting on an empty seat and a pair of lady's high-heeled shoes on the floor that looked as though they'd been kicked off in a hurry.

Wondering as to the whereabouts of the owner of the stilettos, Xhandra looked at the male passenger seated next to the empty seat. He gestured toward the back of the plane. Since he had pointed in the direction of the lavs, Xhandra assumed he meant the mystery person had gone to the bathroom. She didn't think much else about it with all the furor of people asking questions, finding places to stow luggage, and the general process of passengers settling into their seats on a dual aisle airplane, until she got closer to the back.

Xhandra came to one section and realized all the passengers were staring at her with a wide-eyed expression that said *Help!* Something wasn't right, but she couldn't quite put a finger on what had happened. That's when she noticed a shoeless, middle-aged woman in a tight, low-cut dress snuggling all over a much younger man. With two empty seats next to him, there was no reason for the woman to be almost sitting on top of this poor guy. The look of horror on his face showed his discomfort with the situation. Also that he wasn't associated with this woman who was hanging on him and repeating gibberish in Spanish which included, "*Mi amor.*"

"Ma'am, you need to return to your seat," Xhandra said, politely but firmly.

"No, I like this one," the woman said, as if she was picking out a new puppy.

"You need to go back to your seat. Now!" Xhandra insisted.

The wannabe cougar refused to budge, continuing to hug and caress this poor fellow.

Xhandra gave her one more chance. "If you don't go back to your seat immediately, you will be taken off the plane."

The barefoot lady yelled back at her, "You just don't like men. It's not my fault if I'm horny." The lady reluctantly tore herself away from the young man and headed back up the aisle toward her seat.

That's when a female passenger pointed at Xhandra and said, "You need to do something with that lady. She kissed my husband when he came out of the bathroom."

A few minutes later, while doing her compliance checks—seat belts, carry-on-baggage, cell phones, blackberries, blueberries, cranberries, anything with an on-off switch that must be turned off—

Xhandra checked on the crazy lady's seat. Empty again. It seemed she'd never returned to her seat after all. She'd mounted the lap of the poor unrelated man seated next to her, rocking back and forth as though riding a bull in a rodeo.

Xhandra had had enough of this woman's erotic activities so she called the captain to return to the gate so "Ms. Horny Lady" could be taken off the plane. Security escorted the disruptive passenger off the plane as she continued yelling the whole way, "I can't help it if I'm horny!"

As the group marched past the cockpit, the captain glanced at the lady. Getting the first officer's attention, he revved up in his seat and pointed in her direction. "That's her! That's the lady I was telling you about, who was *grabbing ass* right in front of the TSA security."

Then he told the first officer the rest of his story. "I was going through the airport security checkpoint. When it was my turn, I bent over to pick up my bag to put it on the belt of the screening machine. That crazy lady was standing right behind me. She grabbed my butt. I didn't know how to handle it. Then she wouldn't let go. I jumped up but she held on. She batted those fake eyelashes at me and winked, yelling out to everyone in Spanish and English, '*Mi Piloto. Mi Piloto.* My Little Pilot!' "

DRUGS AND AIR TRAVEL DON'T MIX

Drugs and air travel can be a dangerous mix. Perhaps the horny lady in the previous story had taken a dose of female Viagra, because I just can't imagine a rational human being behaving that way.

We finally took off on what seemed like a calm flight. This time I was working in first class with Jennifer, the purser. We settled into our routine, counting down the hours until our layover.

Amy, a crew member working in coach came up front.

"Hey Jen, there's a really weird passenger in the back. During the beverage service and every time a flight attendant passes by he comes out with these outbursts about our airline. He's in an aisle seat towards the middle so he's bothering everyone. Some of it is typical passenger banter—problems with tickets, luggage and other personal nonsense that happened before the flight. You know, nothing out of the ordinary that I haven't heard before. He's a big guy with scraggly blond hair... looks and sounds strange. . I don't feel good about the situation. There's just something about him."

"Which side is he on?"

"Airplane left."

Jennifer tried to reassure her.

"Maybe he just wants to let off some steam, and then he'll quiet down. Keep me posted if it escalates."

"Gotcha. I just wanted all the crew members to be aware of him," Amy said as she turned to go.

Jennifer turned the lights down, to indicate the completion of all services, and I settled into the jump seat for a minute with a snack and a magazine. That's when we heard the yelling. It started as a loud male voice. More loud voices joined in, coming from the back of the plane. A barrage of call lights started going off. Screaming passengers jumped up out of their seats. Flight attendants ran from all directions toward the disturbance.

Jen looked at me as she took off in a hurry. "You stay here and call the captain."

The weird guy had gone berserk. He was thrashing about and hitting the passengers around him. I'd always heard that a drug-induced rage can give a person superhuman strength, but I didn't believe it until that flight. Thank heavens there were two off-duty police officers on board. Three other large male passengers joined them, and it took all of them to subdue him. One man sat on top of him while everyone else gathered various items to restrain him. A passenger volunteered his belt to bind the man's hands, but they still needed to pin down his feet.

Flight attendant George ran to the storage closet in the front and, in his rush to get back, he threw open his zipper bag. George's stash of condoms went flying up in the air, showering the shiny packets of silver, purple, red and blue over several rows of passengers. Thinking he could collect them later, he continued on his objective to get back to the passengers who were holding down the deranged man. George also grabbed the bag of headsets to use the cords to tie around the man's feet. Of course, an emergency landing ensued, and the man was arrested.

Oddly, when George went back up to the front to collect his condoms, he couldn't find any of them. Not one. Apparently, the people sitting there had absconded with all of his stash.

One of the passengers said, "I thought instead of handing out peanuts, this airline was distributing birth control nowadays. Good idea."

We decided that the airline should have an appropriate advertising campaign for this. A discussion ensued between the flight attendants with suggestions about what the new slogan should be.

The up and coming airline

We know why you fly

You're going to enjoy the experience

Your flight to paradise

You ain't seen nothing yet

Fly the friendly way

But we decided Virgin Atlantic Airways has them all beat at innuendo with their slogans throughout the years.

Extra inches where it counts

Love at first flight

Mine's bigger than yours

More experience than our name suggests

You never forget your first time

I'll bet now you'll never see airline slogans the same way again.

Elizabeth Calwell

ALCOHOL AND AIR TRAVEL DON'T MIX EITHER

Dan, also a purser, filled us in on an incident that had happened on one of his previous flights. It involved two well-dressed businessmen seated next to each other in first class, who decided to take advantage of the free alcohol.

"Although they didn't appear to know each other when they boarded," Dan said, "they soon became best buds in a contest to out drink each other. The man seated next to the window eventually went to sleep, or passed out, but awoke when nature called. He climbed over his drinking buddy who had also passed out."

When the soused passenger came out of the lav, Dan happened to be sitting on the jump seat a few feet away. The man rushed over to Dan, turned his head while pointing at the left side of his face, and screamed, "Look at this!"

Dan said, "I saw what looked like a thick black mustache that had been sloppily drawn on the left side of his face. Then the man turned his head the other way; there was no mustache on the right. Apparently, the intoxicated prankster seated next to him drew the

110

mustache on with a permanent black marker; but because his passed out subject was leaning against the window, the drunken seatmate could only draw half a mustache."

Even for Dan, who has an easygoing, down-to-earth personality, and has a great sense of humor, this was too much.

I asked him, "As the purser in charge of the flight, what did you do?"

"Well, the mischievous drunk artist was still soundly asleep, so I found another seat for Mr. Half-mustache. The crew nicknamed him Snidely Whiplash after the old cartoon character with a big handlebar mustache."

I can only imagine Snidely's embarrassment, as he had to walk around in public, not to mention possibly attend important business meetings, decorated like that.

SLEEPLESS IN SEATTLE, OR WHEREVER IT IS THAT I'M LAYING OVER

Once, after a long day, we arrived at our layover hotel. While my fellow crew members and I stood waiting for our room keys at the front counter, a stylishly dressed woman walked up to our captain.

She arrogantly demanded, in a deep, throaty voice, "Take my bags up to room 310."

We all stood there in bewilderment that this person would confuse our captain with a bellman. Not only that, but she picked out the person with the biggest ego in our group, the one most likely to be offended by her remark. Everything went dead silent, as we waited to see his reaction. The look on his face said it all, with his crinkled up forehead and eyes scrunched together.

He replied, without missing a beat, "Do I get to keep the tip?"

At last I settled into my hotel room, after a quick check for bed bugs and perverts. I rested my head on the pillow, while my mind still raced. I tried to tell myself, "Now go to sleep – fast." *Yeah right... like that's ever going to happen. My mind doesn't pay any attention to my ultimatums.*

4:00 a.m.

Drag myself out of bed.

I don't care if you're at home or on a layover, it's human nature not to be able to go to sleep if you have to get up in what is considered the middle of the night. I thought this was caused by my worrying about having to get up at some ungodly hour that prevented me from going to sleep. But it has been scientifically proven that the circadian rhythm, which is the body's natural time-keeping system, dips and rises in a sleep-wake cycle at different times of the day. In adults the strongest sleep drive generally occurs between 2:00-4:00 a.m.

Flight attendants know all about sleep disruption with all-nighter trips, different time zones, and schedules that don't allow for sufficient sleep

However, I really hadn't slept that night because I'd heard all the commotion from the elevators right across the hall from my room all night long. Every time a group of people arrived on my floor, loud footsteps, voices, and slamming of the heavy doors echoed and amplified down the ceramic-tiled hallways.

At one point, two people were yelling to one another from one end of the hallway to the other. I'd had enough. Usually I'm pretty mild-mannered and always security conscious, especially when opening my door to a stranger or who-knows-what in the middle of the night. But this had irritated my last nerve.

Despite the fact that I was in my nighttime glory, in my shorty-nightgown with one roller on top of my head, I got out of bed, flung the door open, and barreled out of my room.

Thinking the disruptive people were at the other end of the hall, I yelled, "Y'all need to be quiet!" as I ran full force right into the noisy guy.

"@#$%!" both of us screamed as we scared each other to death. It turned out that he worked for the hotel and his loud conversation was with another hotel employee at the other end of the hall. He won't be making a disturbance like that again in the middle of the night. I think I frightened the bejesus out of him.

This reminded me of another sleepless night story told by a flight attendant. Wide-awake at 2 a.m., staring at the ceiling, she couldn't sleep because of someone's obnoxious snoring in the adjoining hotel room. Becoming more desperate after having been tortured for hours, she devised a plan. If she called the other room, it would wake up the person long enough for her to go to sleep. Maybe then she could get a couple of hours rest on this short layover.

She heard the phone ring.

When the person answered the phone, she hung up and thought to herself, "Finally some peace and quiet."

Then she heard her neighbor's shower running, followed by the roar of the hair dryer. The door slammed as the person left the room. It turned out it was the captain on her trip. When the phone rang, he thought he'd received his wake up call so he got dressed and headed out.

The next morning, at their actual pick-up time, he was complaining about the fake wake up call. She didn't say a word. She wanted to apologize, but in his irritable state, what could she possibly have said to make matters any better?

THE COMMUNITY WATCH GROUP

Aunt Willa greeted me at the front door that night as I arrived home from a long trip. I knew something was up because she never left her comfortable chair in the den, especially when her favorite show, *Murder She Wrote,* was on TV.

Our usual routine was that Willa would hear the big, clunky lock on the front door, and she would yell, "Elizabeth, is that you?"

"Yes, it's me."

"Where's my Belgian chocolate?"

"I'm comin'. Be there in a minute."

You'd better believe Willa looked forward to her treats. I always brought home chocolates or specialty sweets from wherever I'd been in the world. Tonight though, she looked disturbed and was peeking out the blinds.

"I'm afraid. There's a man out there who's scaring me to death. He's been driving very slowly around the block for hours."

She and the other little old ladies in the neighborhood had kept the phone lines hot. According to Willa, they were convinced he was casing the neighborhood.

Organized watch groups didn't exist at that time. Willa and her friends were the first neighborhood watch group ever. Anytime a break-in or robbery happened in the vicinity, all the neighbors knew about it, just by word of mouth.

Well, I was off the airplane, but now I was on stepped-down security duty for Willa and her pals. I knew, in my exhausted state of mind, there would be no end to this until I got to the bottom of it. I knew this because I was the only person around who was less than one hundred and twenty years old. *Can you tell that I'm tired and cranky?*

I went outside in front of the house and waited until the next time the man came by so I could wave him down. To my surprise, he stopped.

"Excuse me sir, but some of the neighbors keep an eye on what's going on in the neighborhood. I know it's none of my business, but my aunt and her friends were wondering why you've been driving around and around?"

I circled my index finger in the air for emphasis.

He kind of chuckled, and then whispered, while pointing to the back seat, "I'm trying to get my baby to sleep. This is the only thing that works."

Under the glow of the streetlight I could see the sleeping infant in its car seat.

"It's comforting to know that people are watching out." Then the alleged burglar added, "Tell them to keep up the good work."

I reported back to the *Watch Group* and the big excitement for the night was extinguished. This allowed everyone, especially me, to get some much needed sleep.

The next morning I trudged down the stairs for breakfast. Willa could be heard already stirring around, and I smelled the coffee. Sleepwalking into the kitchen, I headed straight for the caffeine. Everything had settled down from the night before, so Willa finally got around to asking me about my trip.

"So where'd you go? Tell me all about it."

"It was a good trip, except for one problem." I blew on my hot coffee.

"Why? What happened?" Willa looked concerned because I usually had something exciting or interesting to tell about my adventures.

"Well, we were in the middle of our beverage service on the last leg. You know we often run out of certain sodas as we approach the back. So, in the next row of passengers there was a young child, maybe seven years old, seated in the middle next to her mother on the aisle side.

The child looked like a Mini-Me of the mother with shoulder-length, curly, dark hair. The only difference was that the mother had on the biggest pair of dark-rimmed glasses I've ever seen. I politely asked the child what she wanted to drink. She just sat there, didn't acknowledge me, or even look up from her game.

"Now Willa, you gotta picture this. I'm standing there in the aisle with a person waiting right behind me to go to the bathroom, literally right on my butt. I don't know why people feel like they've got to get so close. Usually I don't even know someone's breathing down my neck until I bend over to retrieve a soda out of the cart and accidentally butt 'em outta my way. Anyway, we were in a hurry to get the cart out of the aisle. After repeating my request again to the child, the mother blurted out, 'Ginger Ale.'

"I told them that we were out of ginger ale, but we did have Sprite. This set off a spark under that child. She looked up and put on such a dramatic act of rolling, not only her eyes, but also her head in a huge circle, all the while puffing out with a big audible sigh."

"Really." Willa raised her eyebrows. "A little kid did that? What was her problem?"

"I don't know. You would've thought I'd just said something awful or, much worse, interrupted her game."

"I know that I would've said something." Willa shook her head. "I'd never be able to do your job."

"Well, I did. I said something, all right. And that's the problem. I looked at the mother and said, just as nicely as I could, in a joking manner, 'You know, *she* is way too young to be displaying an attitude like that,' then I chuckled to show that I was kidding, sort of.

Oops. Dead silence. The mother didn't think it was funny.

"Willa, I couldn't help it. It just came flying out of my mouth. I thought I probably crossed the line with that one. I could have gotten in big trouble."

"Elizabeth, you need to learn to pick your battles. I don't think that little kid was worth it. Then what happened?"

Willa folded up the *New York Times* pages to get the crossword puzzle ready.

"The mother got really defensive. You know, like mother, like daughter. Her eyes narrowed behind those big glasses. She scrunched up her nose and pursed her lips like the wicked witch in the *Wizard of Oz*. Extending a long bony finger, she pointed at the child, and, talking through her teeth, she said, 'He's a boy.' "

Willa gasped as she laughed out loud. "You're kidding. What happened?"

"Well. This caught me so off-guard! All I could come out with was, 'Oops. Uh. Oh. OK.' Then the little boy rolled his eyes again, like I should have known better. I just handed the child, who still hadn't spoken a word, a Sprite. I've had a great deal of practice in keeping a straight face but I'll tell you right now that I lost it. I stepped on that brake pedal and moved that cart as fast as I could go."

Willa listened intently as I vented, and then laughed. "I don't blame you at all. Manners are manners no matter whether it's a boy or a girl. That's what that lady gets for raising a child that doesn't say please or thank you. There's no excuse for parents to allow a child to get away with being rude."

Uh oh, I've started Willa on one of her rampages.

I nodded. "My generation was taught to respect adults. If I'd acted like that, my mama would've shot me one of those 'looks,' that my cousin Carl calls 'the stink-eye.' He should know because he gets 'em all the time from his wife, Lisa. I even catch myself doing it from time to time."

"What did your buddies on the airplane think about that?"

"They all got a kick out of it and laughed, just another typical day on the airplane."

I cut two pieces of Entenmann's coffee cake and passed one to Willa. "I wish that kid, and his mother too, could see some of the poor, deprived children I've seen."

Willa was wound up now. "When your Uncle Buck and I visited Africa, we saw extreme poverty everywhere. A guide took me to the market to buy trinkets, but I wouldn't bargain for anything. I just paid whatever they asked. They needed the money more than I did. The guide got upset with me. He explained that the vendors want to haggle. It's part of the process."

"Wow! Willa, that sounds like some of the places I've been, like some of my first trips to Santo Domingo. The crew and I came out of the airport heading to the van and some small boys, no more than about five years old, were waiting. They pleaded with us to shine our shoes for a dollar. None of them had a shoeshine kit either. They carried a homemade concoction of Lord-knows-what in one hand, and a dirty cloth in the other. Since they weren't allowed to beg at the airport, this was how they made money. These little boys with callused feet and dirty faces looked up at me with those sad eyes. I always got my shoes shined. Sometimes I had one kid shining the right shoe and another one shining the left shoe and I paid them each a dollar or two. We did the same trip all month, and I saw those same children every time, whether we left late at night or early in the morning.

"My friend Miguel, who's from the Dominican Republic, warned me, 'Don't ever give money to any of the children who are begging, because the money usually goes to some adult for drugs or alcohol.'"

I later found out that it was a sad but hard truth, but I couldn't just do nothing. I started bringing lots of flip-flops for the barefoot kids, and real shoeshine equipment. At least this encouraged them to find work shining shoes. Some of the children would chase after our van begging for money and came so close that a couple of them almost got run over. It got to be so dangerous that the authorities banned them from the airport. Those children are still a vivid memory. I just felt so bad for them, living the way they do.

Willa said, "Kids today don't realize how lucky they are to live in the U.S."

"I know some do. Just the other day I was talking with a lady on my flight about this. She and her family were returning from a mission trip in Honduras helping to build a school. I asked if her kids had ever seen poverty like that before. She told me they'd never seen anything even close to the deprivation those poor people lived in. Then she added, the trip made an impact that will last for the rest of their lives."

DUELING PENISES

(I had to look that word up. I've never seen it in plural before.)

After I finished breakfast, I told Willa, "I've got to run. Gonna grab a movie at Blockbuster before they run out of the good ones. You mentioned your friend from the church was coming over to join us tonight."

Every once in a while, I would rent a movie for us to watch. On this night my Aunt Willa had invited her friend, who was also far along in years, to come join us. I ran into Blockbuster Video and asked the young man behind the counter for a recommendation.

"I'm in the mood for a comedy."

"You gotta watch this one." He handed me a video. "It's a hoot."

Running behind time, I took his suggestion, grabbed *Skin Deep,* and headed for home. Mrs. Velnick came over that night and we settled down to watch the movie. I snuggled in on one end of the couch with an afghan, as the frail gray-haired church lady sat up very prim and proper on the other end. Willa nestled into her easy chair with the ottoman.

The movie went along just fine until…

"Whoa!" I sat straight up. *Oh shit! That's not a…oh no!*

Willa squinted and moved forward in her chair. "Is that what I think it is?"

Mrs. Velnick threw her hands up in the air.

"Oh, my word," she said in a high-pitched voice and then laughed.

I didn't dare look at her.

The two guys in the movie were wearing glow-in-the-dark condoms. They were in a pitch-black room, dueling with their penises! I thought I would die of embarrassment, not because of the movie but because of the company I was with. Just picture, two elderly ladies, and me watching a risqué movie together!

Believe it or not, they both laughed and whooped it up the whole time. They actually enjoyed it.

When Mrs. Velnick got up to leave she looked at me and said, "You need to go back to that section in the video store. I've definitely never seen anything like that before."

Willa looked at both of us with a twinkle in her eye.

"Wow, I can't wait to tell my bridge club about those shenanigans."

"Y'all, it really was not an X-rated movie."

They looked at each other and said at the same time, "Yeah, right."

"I didn't pick it out; the guy at Blockbuster did."

"Yeah, right."

⤞　　　⤝

The next day I went to Naomi's house to borrow a book that she'd told me about. When I knocked on her door, she opened it wide.

"Come on in. Have a cup of coffee?"

"Sure. I'd love one. I need some caffeine." Naomi led the way to the kitchen table.

"Where did you go on your trip this time?" Naomi shoved a plate of brownies at me as we sat down, knowing that I can't resist chocolate.

"San Antonio. We didn't go see the Alamo, but we took a boat ride on the San Antonio River that circles through downtown. It was so much fun."

"I've been there. It's been awhile, but I remember the beautiful river walk with all its restaurants." Naomi poured another cup of coffee.

"We had seven flight attendants in our group; five of them spoke other languages. So when we passed another boat full of people, we all started speaking in different languages as if we were into a serious conversation. We got the weirdest stares. People gawked at us trying to figure out what country we were from. We had a blast."

'You don't speak a foreign language."

"No, I just made up some foreign-sounding gibberish. My cousin, Nikki, taught me how to do it. All you have to do is clear the back of your throat like you have a hairball, while you end every word with 'icktch' 'ento' or 'stein.' Everyone said I did a pretty good job."

"I bet those people you passed really couldn't figure out which country *you* were from."

"Ya got that right."

'Does Nikki speak a foreign language?"

"Oh hell no. She only speaks Southern – like me."

This brought a snicker from Naomi, and she went on in her native Lawng Island accent. "You know, your Aunt Willa is really lucky to have you here. Her daughters have been pushing her to move into a retirement home and Lord knows she does not want to move, even though she needs to be thinking seriously about it."

"Are you kidding? I'm the lucky one, especially while adjusting to this new unconventional lifestyle, far away from family, friends, and my old stomping grounds. Believe it or not, a lot of people didn't know what being a flight attendant entailed when they accepted the job. Including me. They're here in New York without an Aunt Willa in their life."

She offered to refill my cup.

"Thanks Naomi. No more coffee for me. That's enough reminiscing for today. I've got to go do laundry for my trip tomorrow."

"Oh shoot. I was hoping we could go shopping."

"Yeah, me too." *Brownies and no exercise. If I keep this up, I'll be as big as a house.*

BOOBS

I couldn't wait to call Renea. Remember her? She was at the original luncheon with Anne that got me into this wacky lifestyle. Renea has been my best friend forever, and she's the other person besides Aunt Willa that I can vent and share funny stories with.

We have a birthday card we pass back and forth to each other, and it says: 'We know too much about each other not to be friends.'

I called Renea. The phone rang and she answered, "Hello."

"Hey Renea, I'm glad you're home."

"Uh oh. What happened on your flight this time?"

"You're just not going to believe the shit that happens on these airplanes. I couldn't make this stuff up if I tried. You'd better sit down for this one."

"OK, I'm ready." I could hear Renea pulling up a chair. "Go ahead. What happened?"

"We were delayed on the taxi out, and the captain came on the PA to say that we wouldn't be taking off for another twenty minutes. I was already in my jump seat facing the passengers when a male flight attendant walked past me, heading toward the back of the plane. He stopped and did a double take at the lady sitting diagonally across from me because she had fallen asleep while breastfeeding. She had one rather large breast flopped out on the aisle side and a baby hanging out the other side. I hadn't noticed, since I was giving her some privacy so I had turned in the other direction talking with another passenger. Seeing the astonished look on his face, I jumped up, retrieved a blanket and laid it over her discreetly.

"Later during the flight, I couldn't wait to go up front to rib John, the male flight attendant, about his reaction. He told me that he has seen so many boobs on airplanes he couldn't even keep count.

"John told me about the time he was offering pre-departure drinks in first class on a 767 flight to London. Very carefully, he balanced a full tray of glasses with champagne, orange juice, and water, as he headed toward a lady in a white shirt with a big, poofed-up French twist hairdo. Someone behind him backed into him just when he offered her a drink, making him tilt the whole tray of drinks on top of the lady's head. She was *not* a happy camper.

She started screaming, going off in a rage before running into the lav to try to wash off as much of the sticky mess before her six-hour flight. She had been gone for a while when the same male flight attendant went to go into the lav, not knowing the lady was still in there. She hadn't locked the door. He opened the door to find her totally naked from the waist up. Without any other change of clothes, she had taken off her blouse and bra to rinse them out. She started yelling that he was harassing her, and that this was the worst trip she'd ever been on, and on, and on, and on."

Renea laughed as she said, "Whoa, what a mess."

"Yeah but this fiasco happened before they had even taken off. He still had to work in first class with her the whole flight."

"Oh no. That's awful."

"Wait, it gets worse. Are you still sitting down? Then, on another occasion, John was the purser again. He was working first class when he got a call from the back of the plane because a lady was breastfeeding. The upset flight attendant on the phone demanded that the purser needed to get back there and handle it. John told the flight attendant in the back that breastfeeding was a natural thing, and to get a grip."

"I'm glad he did. The breast feeding support groups would not appreciate that other person's attitude." Renea finally got in her two cents worth.

"No, this was different. When he went to the back of the plane the lady was breast-feeding a dog. A dog. I don't need to say anymore except that he told her if she did it again she would be removed from the plane."

"Eww! That's disgusting. You're right. There's no way you could make this shit up."

"Oh, and this one happened to me recently. These two girls came onto the plane wearing bikini tops and short shorts. They'd been drinking before they came on and were having a good time. Once we were in the air, one of the girls played a prank on her friend. She undid the back snap on the other girl's bathing suit. The girl's big boobs came bursting out and smacked the tray table in front of her.

"The captain and I are good friends, so as kind of a joke, I called him to find out what we should do, or if *he* wanted to handle the situation himself. This was back before 9/11 when the pilots could come out whenever they wanted. By way of an answer, the cockpit door flung open, and he shot out of there like a racehorse out of the gate. He was determined to handle the disruptive passenger."

Renea said, "Let's see…stay in a boring cockpit or…Yeah, I'll bet y'all were taking bets to see how long that would take."

CALLED OUT ON RESERVE FOR A RIO TRIP

Imagine it's ten o'clock at night and I haven't been to sleep since the previous night when normal people (like you) sleep.

The phone rang at Aunt Willa's house.

I ran downstairs and answered it. "Hello."

A crisp voice said, "Is this flight attendant Calwell?"

"Yes it is."

"This is crew schedule. We have a trip for you."

My response came out automatically without even thinking about getting into trouble. "Is this legal? I mean, to be on call twenty-four seven. I know I'm on reserve but this is unreal."

No reaction from crew schedule about my comment.

"You're the number five position, on a trip to Rio. You need to step on it. You only have two hours to get to the airport."

Oh shit, Rio de Janeiro is a nine-hour flight. I'm going to die.

I paused. "O...K..."

I hustled and barely made it on time to catch the employee bus to the airport from the parking lot. I spotted another flight attendant already seated, so I flung my bags in the rack and sat down.

Thinking no one else would be on the bus this late except flight attendants leaving on trips, I asked her, "Are you going to Rio?"

"Yes."

"Hi. My name's Elizabeth."

"I'm Jacqueline."

Jacqueline pulled out a mirror to add some gloss to her bright red lipstick and then patted her perfectly styled hairdo. She could have been a Whitney Houston look-alike. Her tall, thin stature did justice to the uniform for an elegant, well put together appearance. Even from a few seats away, I detected an attitude about having to leave for work at this hour.

Looking for a little sympathy myself, I attempted to make conversation.

"I just got called out on reserve to be the first class galley flight attendant. I've never done it before."

"You've never been the galley flight attendant?" Her inquisition dripped with the tone of an all-knowing senior mama.

"No." I shook my head. *Oh shit, if this is what it's going to be like then I'm in trouble.*

"Do you know what all you have to do?" She started counting off her fingers the list of duties expected of the galley flight attendant.

"Crack all the bags of ice, set up the beverage carts, set up the inserts for pre-departure beverages, count the meals and determine the quantity of each different entrée, check all supplies, count the cockpit meals separately, set up a three-tiered cart for appetizers, and another one for the salad service, and another one for desserts"

She stopped for a breath and rolled her eyes.

"If you're missing any supplies, you need to order replacements quickly from catering. A few missing items can make the whole meal service a disaster."

With my luck, we'll probably be missing something like plates or silverware. I wouldn't find out about it until we were halfway to Rio, when all the first class passengers start screaming at me. I would be able to handle this if I wasn't so tired.

"Oh yeah, and all of this is accomplished with five thousand people running through the galley asking you questions."

Most passengers just assume that when we arrive on the plane everything is already set up for us. Nothing could be further from the truth. All the supplies are mummy-wrapped in plastic, in boxes and hidden in every available crevice and cart. The first class galley position always goes to a senior flight attendant familiar with all the work required to get everything organized before departure and during the flight.

I sat there in bewilderment, and she kept talking. I morphed into Charlie Brown from the comics. All I heard was *blah, blah, blah, blah, blah*. She spewed out more instructions. "If you have any special… only have two ovens… take everything out of one oven to cook a… but you won't know about that until the last minute."

What? This is going to be a disaster.

"OK." I'd totally given up on taking mental notes.

She continued spouting. "Did you know you have to hand plate and dish out each dinner for thirty people, besides keeping the flow of the entire four-course meal service going?"

Ugh, that's going to be a mess. A mental image appeared of me slinging hash.

"You have got to be kidding. Anything else?" *I was afraid to ask.*

"Yes," she said, not even taking a breath. "For the breakfast service in the morning, you have to cook eggs to order."

Wow, if I make it to breakfast it'll be a miracle.

"That's OK, I can handle eggs. Everyone will get them scrambled." *What do they think we are? Gourmet cooks?*

She had obviously done this service many times. Now she was looking at me with pity. "Are you new?"

"Yes, brand new. I've never even set foot on this airplane before. Not only that, but I went home for six weeks after training, because of the Gulf War, before I actually started working. Everything I learned about food prep turned into a blur."

She threw in the final grenade.

"I know the purser you'll be working with. She's going to chew you up and spit you out."

"Oh great, I can't wait."

During initial training we worked on simulated airplane mock-ups, with a focus on emergency procedures. All the food service training was pretend. We never cooked real food, much less eggs. That particular menu item didn't last very long. It was a disaster. The passengers woke up in the morning and wanted their eggs cooked perfectly to each individual preference. Don't these people know that the air pressure at high altitude will cause food to cook differently than usual? Have you ever noticed the high altitude instructions on the back of a box of cake mix? I bet the cake mix wasn't referring to 35,000 feet.

We arrived at the airport, and I dragged my bags off the bus. Jacqueline waited for me and we headed to Ops together, to sign in.

Taking a deep breath, I told myself this wasn't going to kill me. However, I was starting to have my doubts. My mama always said, 'Stop worrying yourself. Ninety-five percent of what you worry about never happens. The other five percent, there's nothing you can do about it.'

Just before we reached Ops, Jacqueline turned to me

"OK, I'll trade positions with you."

"Can we do that?" I couldn't believe it.

"Yeah, we'll have to get permission from crew schedule, because you're on reserve."

"Oh my gosh! Jacqueline, you're an angel. Thank you so much."

Jacqueline wore a mischievous grin.

"Sorry 'bout letting you squirm. It's bad enough to be on reserve. Besides, working the first class galley is the most demanding position on the plane. I can't believe crew schedule won't help y'all out in any shape, form, or fashion."

I ended up working a non-galley position in coach with a sympathetic crew. To this day, I'm still thankful to Jacqueline for helping me out. And as usual, Mama was right. Bless her soul.

STRIP SHOW IN RIO

This was my first trip to Rio. Determination to see some of this new destination was the driving force that got me up and out after being called out on reserve for this all-night assignment. After catching a couple of hours of shut-eye, I forced myself to go sightseeing.

Nobody will ever call me a 'Slam-clicker,' that's what the flight attendants were called who slammed their hotel room door, and clicked the lock, never to be seen again during the entire layover. They were also called 'Olympic Flames' because they never went out, and 'Noodle Crew' because they stayed in the room eating instant noodles.

My Rio crew had decided to meet at an outside café down the street from the hotel. After all the warnings about not going out alone, it was a little nerve-wracking walking along the beach by myself, but I didn't go too far before spotting a couple of my crew members sitting at a rustic picnic table under a thatched roof.

The café turned out to be more like a shack. This quaint location overlooking the beach on the outskirts of the huge, modern city of Rio, also served as the gathering place for the locals. I enjoyed the seaside scenery, and in my sleepy state would've been happy to stay right there, just looking at the water, people watching, and enjoying the breeze.

The flight attendants started arriving, including Paulo, one of our Portuguese speakers. We designated Paulo as our fearless leader, since the majority of his work trips were to Rio. He knew where to go and how to get there. Paulo and the others started discussing where we should go for dinner. Jim, our captain, joined us and sat next to me on the sidewalk side of the table.

While waiting for the rest of the crew to arrive, a little boy came up, begging to shine our shoes. I always fall hard for the big brown eyes, and I motioned for him to go ahead, although my shoes weren't the right kind of shoes. He started shinning away, with a wide smile of appreciation in hope of being paid even a little bit of money.

At the same time his little arm was flying side-to-side, he looked up at me and swiped a big black streak of shoe polish right across the top of my foot. Paulo scolded him, in Portuguese, to be more careful. The little boy's facial expression changed; he was now afraid he wouldn't be paid. Of course, I paid him. I didn't say a word about my new trend in body art with the black-striped foot.

"Do I look like the soft-hearted person in the group, or the sucker? Why do they always come up to me?" I asked.

"You're not the only one." Jim handed me a napkin, but it didn't help. The black stuff dries fast.

He said, "They get me too. On my last trip, a youngster started following me around. When I went into a store, he waited for me outside. After he trailed me for a few blocks, I realized he was barefoot and asked him if he wanted some shoes, pointing to a regular pair of sneakers in a store window. The boy said, '*Muito obrigado*' (thank you very much), and I escorted him into the store.

"Wouldn't you know the first pair of tennis shoes that he picked up had the lights across the heel? I wasn't planning on spending that much money, but if you'd seen the boy's face. He had never seen anything as marvelous as those tennis shoes in his whole life. So I bought them for him."

"I hope he got to keep the shoes," said Paulo.

Another crew member said, "Yeah, the older kids probably beat him up and took them away from him."

"Well, at least he had something special." Jim shrugged. "Even if only for a short time."

I gave Paulo, and the other guy, an annoyed look for saying such an awful thing. "I hope he hid his new shoes from those other mean kids. I don't want to think about what happened."

We decided to go exploring. We jumped into two taxis to meet at a restaurant, which ended up being on the other side of the city. After finishing dinner, our fearless leader and some of the others decided we should check out the male strip show right across the street. We all thought it would be fun, like the Chippendale male strip shows in the United States.

However, the captain had been led to believe that it was a female strip show. He didn't know until we got there that it was a male strip show. He came in with us anyway, because it was a long way back by taxi. I just went along with the crew. I knew it was bound to be an interesting experience, one way, or another.

Once inside the theater, all eight of us sat in one row toward the front. We had a great view. Every time the MC told a joke, Paolo, our Portuguese speaker, would translate and it would be passed down the row, from one person to another. At least Jim enjoyed some of the performance with the jokes and the music. This spectacular show compared to the striptease shows in the U.S., except in Rio they eventually peeled off all of their clothes, as in totally nude. As we would say in North Carolina, totally 'neked.'

The grand finale was when two of the 'neked' guys came walking out simultaneously from opposite sides of the stage.

I thought they were carrying swords.

When I told Aunt Willa this story she said, "Swords…really!" and gave me that look.

THE PASSENGER WHISPERER

The morning beverage service is the most challenging for flight attendants. I'm not the only one who feels this way, because there was an article in *Reader's Digest* depicting this as the ultimate pet peeve for flight attendants on all airlines. Along with my fellow workers, I refer to it as the 'deer-in-headlights' service.

A perfect example is a recent morning's beverage service on a full flight.

I began with the first passenger, a look-alike of Benjamin Franklin.

I mustered up a smile, despite the pre-dawn hour, and asked, "What would you like to drink?"

Mr. Ben Franklin, who had a receding hairline and glasses propped on the end of his nose, sat there with a blank stare.

"Excuse me, sir," I asked politely, "would you like to have something to drink this morning?"

Mr. Franklin, still with a bovine gaze in his eyes, mumbled, "Coffee."

"What would you like in your coffee?" I wanted to hold up the milk and say, "Moo" just to get through to him.

'Just coffee.'

I repeated, "A black coffee?"

He nodded. So I handed him a cup of black coffee. I moved on to the next row. Mr. Franklin called back to me, "Hey, where's my cream?"

I returned, added milk to his coffee, and then started to help the next passengers, now two rows further back.

"Hey, I need sugar!" he yelled louder.

Deep down, I wanted to show him my fastball with a five-pound bag of sugar, but I managed to keep my cool. Besides, my semilethargic self just wanted to give him the sugar and move on. For the remainder of the service, this scenario played out over and over and over, with an airplane full of catatonic sleepwalkers.

That is until I got to 24C, where a woman answered sweetly and sincerely, "A cappuccino, please!"

"Certainly! Just a minute," I said with a grin. "Hey A.B., we have a request for a cappuccino. Will you take care of it?"

A.B., who is a big, teddy bear of a guy, looked up with a friendly smile. I knew handling this just happened to be his specialty.

Of course, we don't have a cappuccino machine on the beverage cart but that was never a problem for A.B. He loved going overboard while having fun with the passengers. He held the coffee pot up high above the cup, and as he poured he made the sound of a cappuccino machine, "kapush-kapush-kapush." Then, he pretended to be pulling down on a big handle.

Because he was standing in the middle of the aisle, A.B. had captured the attention of several rows of passengers by the time he finished and handed the lady—a regular coffee. She roared with laughter right along with the other passengers and enjoyed being part of the show.

The first time I flew with A.B. he introduced himself in an easygoing manner with a slight accent.

"Just call me A.B. I'm from Italy, and no one can remember my real name." The four or five languages he spoke fluently often came in handy when situations arose with non-English speaking passengers. Before working for the airline, A.B. had worked all over the world in several different careers – once as a professional magician. Working with him definitely kept our job interesting. Most of the time he entertained me with his magic tricks, right along with the passengers. We all tried to figure out how he pulled a quarter out of a child's ear or made a coin disappear.

His small audience had enjoyed his performance but then I had to be the one who kept the beverage service moving, so I pulled the cart back another few rows. My next passenger was a sunburned, stringy-blond guy wearing a tee shirt with 'Boobies Make Me Smile' on it. He had on his noise-canceling Bose headset so he couldn't hear anything, including me. I waved to get his attention, and pointed to my invisible headset. He didn't take the hint.

I have learned to work with headset-wearing passengers by moving my lips without saying anything. I mime as if I'm having a serious discussion with them. This usually works to lure the person to take off their headset, because then they think they've gone deaf.

But this time my game didn't work, and he screamed out, "What? What did you say?"

With the next passenger I tried a different approach, "Would you like something to drink?"

The passenger replied with a curt, "Yes," followed with a deliberate dead silence and a fixed look at me, as though I was supposed to read his mind. I raised my eyebrows and pointed to the orange juice.

As the morning wore on, and after a few more of these encounters, I tried to make the decision process go a little faster. I held up a cup of orange juice as a suggestion and a lot of people nodded their heads in agreement. It's usually OJ or coffee in the morning, so this eliminated fifty percent of the decision-making process. The passengers seemed grateful for not having to think with their low battery brainpower that early in the morning.

I've never seen men or women having any trouble making up their minds anywhere else. If this beverage service took place in a bar, a guy, without hesitation, would've placed a complicated drink order, and then left a tip. James Bond ordered his drinks with precise instructions.

"Vodka Martini, shaken not stirred."

So exactly what is it about being on an airplane that causes people to zombie-out like some supernatural force has put them in a trance?

I'm an amiable person, but even for me, this early morning beverage service has always felt like some kind of passenger-induced torture treatment. I don't think the water-drip method could be any worse than the *deer-in-headlights* coffee service.

Finally, we got to the last row. This businessman was my buddy, whom I'd helped quite a bit in getting settled during boarding. But once again, I got the *bovine bumpkin stare.*

"Coffee? Cream? Sugar?"

I calculated I'd repeated this same question over a hundred times, just on this one flight. Multiply that by fifteen to twenty days a month over twenty-five years, and I've dealt with the deer-in-headlights question well over 250,000 times.

After quite a pause, my buddy said, "Just coffee."

And the response was no different with this Mr. Million-Mile (Star Alliance, Platinum, Medallion, Sky Miles) business passenger on the last row.

"Do you want anything in your coffee?"

"Cream."

"A coffee with just cream?"

'And sugar."

As I was handing him some packets of sugar, he blurted out "No. Equal," as if I should have known better.

That was the straw that broke *this* camel's back. I gave him 'the stink-eye look' and said, "Now you've told me you fly a million-plus miles a year. You had to get this ticket at the last minute, that's why you're on the last row. Correct?"

He replied apprehensively, "Yes."

"How many years have you been drinking coffee?" *I was thinking more than forty.*

I didn't wait for his answer; I scolded him in my light-hearted manner. "You fly enough that you should know better than to make me ask twenty questions to find out what you want in your coffee, young man."

Jokingly pointing a disciplinary finger at him, I continued, "You're probably the same guy that goes into a Starbucks and yells out your order of, 'A double espresso, Frappuccino, light, blended, hold the whip, and give me some drizzle.'

In Starbucks you wouldn't dare to falter for a second or you would be crucified by the other customers for holding up their time and their orders."

He said, "You're so right."

I winked at him. "From now on, when a flight attendant asks you, 'What do you want to drink?' your answer is going to be 'Coffee, with cream, and two Equals.' Got it?"

"OK, I got it." He nodded.

I wouldn't have picked on him if I hadn't already talked to him earlier, when I helped him find space for his bags at the last minute. I was venting on him, and he knew it, but what the heck – I felt better and he enjoyed the attention.

My cousin Gena was on a flight when a passenger handed the cup of coffee back and said, "I only wanted half a cup." So the flight attendant took a cup and tore off the top half then put coffee in it and handed it back. I would have to say that that flight attendant had reached her limit.

I still don't know how it is that passengers think we can read their minds. Now, that's a scary thought.

VODKA AS A CURE-ALL FOR WHAT AILS YOU...REeeaLLY?

After completing that morning's beverage service, we'd sat down on our jump seats in the back galley for all of two seconds, when a man came to me for help. He was German and spoke a little English. He explained that his wife wasn't feeling well, as he patted his chest. Along with my two co-workers who were listening, I prepared to spring into action if this really was a heart attack situation.

I started asking medical questions. "Is she diabetic?"

"No."

"Does she have a history of heart problems?"

"No." He shook his head.

"Is she having difficulty breathing?"

In his thick German accent, he answered, "No," to all of these questions. Then he said, in a serious and concerned tone, "She needs vodka."

"Whew."

All three of us breathed a sigh of relief and relaxed as we came out of medical rescue mode.

But the passenger still looked worried as he folded his hands together and repeated, "She needs some vodka for her stomach."

Now he made it clear that he considered vodka a medical remedy. Maybe it works. In my childhood, there was a common sore throat remedy of bourbon mixed with lemon and honey. I know that worked.

Nevertheless, I had to inform him that we don't normally provide vodka to someone who wasn't feeling well.

"No?"

"No. I'm sorry." I shook my head.

I went to check on his wife. Apparently, she had eaten something that didn't agree with her. She was suffering from a bad case of indigestion, along with the pressure of being on an airplane. She was in a lot of pain. But she would be OK…no heart attacks here.

I later learned that vodka mixed with red wine and cranberry juice has been recommended as a home remedy, effective for relieving a cramped or upset stomach. Add a few more ingredients, and this recipe sounds similar to Sangria. Do you think, maybe, Sangria was invented to counter the effects of a spicy meal?

I wish we could give vodka to every passenger. Think about it: everyone would be in a better mood and enjoy their flight.

Hey…maybe a shot for each flight attendant too. (Just kidding.)

I've given you an idea of the typical morning coffee service... and an averted medical emergency. Two hours down, and only eight more to go in this workday, or it could go up to a sixteen-hour day with delays, reassignments, reschedules, de-icing, blizzards, diversions, and/or canceled flights. We never know.

Now, on to the next leg of our three-day trip.

IN THE AIR

SPEAKING OF AIR -
CLEAR AIR FLATULENCE

On this flight, I happened to be walking up the aisle from the back of the plane, when I passed a small boy who started yelling in my direction, "Hey lady! Hey lady!"

I spun around before he woke up too many people and hurried over to his seat. With my index finger to my mouth, I whispered, "Shhhhhh, you need to lower your voice so you don't disturb the people around you. Do you need something?"

"Yes, this airplane farted!" he said loudly, not understanding the concept of talking quietly.

I couldn't help but laugh, right along with everyone else in the vicinity. Now trying to contain a mirthful smile unsuccessfully, I attempted to sound sincere.

"Did you hear something, or did you smell something?"

"I smell something awful," he said with his nose all scrunched up.

I showed him how to open his air vent by twisting the knob counter-clockwise, and assured him, "Whatever you smelled will go away soon." Then I noticed his poor father on the other side, who had attempted to hide with one hand over his forehead and had slid halfway down in his seat. Apparently, he had done an SBD (Silent but Deadly) and thought he could get away with it. Not going to happen, with the Pootn'-Tootn' cheerleader sitting next to him.

I'm surprised this incident embarrassed the man. Most men love farting, and especially stories or jokes about farting. It's a 'man thing.' Flight attendants refer to a fart on the airplane as *crop dusting*. Hey, everybody has to do it sometime, and the air pressure on the plane makes matters worse.

One time, a male flight attendant was standing in the front of the plane during boarding. Only a few passengers had trickled in through the door when suddenly he got the impending urge to break wind. He desperately needed to get rid of this gas before the rest of the passengers came onto the plane. So he backed into the folding door of the lav, which slid open just enough for him to shove his rear end into the space while he stood outside. He bent over and ripped a big one that would've made any man proud. Unbeknownst to him, an older lady had gone into the lav and hadn't locked the door.

The *Agent Orange* victim shot out of the lav faster than a jackrabbit. She glared up and down the aisle looking for the identity of the navy-blue pants that had violated her air space. By this time, the male flight attendant had high-tailed it to the back galley.

An innocent female crew member now standing outside the lav honestly didn't know (until later), why the ranting woman was so angry.

Moral of this story: lock the door. And forget about clear air turbulence. You never can tell when you might encounter *Clear Air Flatulence*. It's worse.

It wasn't just coach passengers who experienced the poison gas ploy. Once, when I was working first class on an Airbus, I discovered this airplane in particular facilitated more abdominal relief than usual.

We were still at the gate when in walked a passenger who would qualify as one of the few genuine bad apples I've ever met. Mr. Attitude began by complaining out loud about all the problems that had happened to him previous to this flight. His actions and body language reeked of a bad disposition. He slammed his bag in the overhead bin then arrogantly stood in the middle of the aisle, holding up everyone trying to board, taking his time as he rummaged through his briefcase.

Once up in the air, his grumbling continued. Flight attendant Kim fixed him a second cup of coffee because the sugar didn't taste right. Then his glass of water had two ice cubes but he only wanted one. He went on and on.

Kim said, "Can you imagine being his wife? Nobody could live with Mr. Personality."

I commiserated with my crew.

"We've got another two hours with this man. We'd better make the best of it."

A male flight attendant, who shall remain unnamed, came up to visit from the back of the plane, and overheard our comments.

Narrowing his eyes he said, "What seat is that man in?"

"3H. Why?"

With a mischievous look, the flight attendant didn't say a word; he did an about-face, walked over to 3H, and just stood there. The rest of us peeked out from behind the curtain, watching curiously from the galley.

Kim said, "What's he doing?"

Then he just casually strolled on off toward the back, as if nothing had happened.

As soon as he left, a ripple of action exploded on the right side of the plane. The passengers all started popping up like gopher heads as they looked up from their books and magazines with frowns and crinkled up noses. One lady pinched her nose with her thumb and index finger as if she just smelled the most disgusting odor she had ever encountered. People grabbed their safety briefing cards to fan themselves as they gasped for air. That flight attendant had *crop-dusted* the man in 3H! Unfortunately the rest of the passengers were collateral damage.

Just when 3H thought he had had the last word, we showed him a thing or two with our flight attendant secret weapon of mass olfactory destruction.

This is a warning – don't mess with a flight attendant.

WORKING IN A PRESSURE COOKER
PRESSURIZATION CHANGES
AND OTHER AILMENTS

Some days I really do feel like I'm working in a pressure cooker.

Aunt Willa had planned another luncheon date with her long-time cronies, and this time we met at a local restaurant in the small downtown area of Manhasset. Naomi's bright green blouse made it easy to spot the group, and we greeted her, along with Ethel, Mary Ann, and Pat and sat down.

Pat turned to me right away and said, "Elizabeth, I'm going on vacation to Europe. Do you have any suggestions for the long flight?"

"I sure do. When you go into the lav, lock the bathroom door."

Everyone gave me a strange look.

"I'm serious. During my last trip, two of us were sitting on the jump seat in front of first class. We were on a 727 airplane, which has a lav adjacent to our jump seat, literally an arms-length away. This double jump seat is mounted on the wall. When you pull it down, you have to sit down quickly or it retracts back up against the wall. We'd just started gobbling down our lunch, with our trays balanced precariously on our laps, when the plane hit some rough turbulence, and began bouncing around rigorously. Wouldn't you know it; the lady in the lav hadn't locked the door. Kerpow! She flew out of the bathroom like a circus clown shot out of a cannon, did a somersault, and landed on the floor in front of our feet with big thud."

"Ooh wee! Was she hurt?" Willa said. "I bet that must have been embarrassing."

"No, not too much. The lady had on a long, flowing skirt so her gymnastic feat wasn't as bad as it could've been. She wasn't hurt but definitely embarrassed."

Mary Ann offered her grandmotherly advice with a wink. "You need to start wearing football gear just to be able eat your dinner."

"What a great idea. I wish we could." I smiled and looked at Pat, repeating my warning, "So be sure and lock the door."

"I always do, but I'll definitely double check it now. Anything else?"

"Yeah, watch what you eat before you get on an airplane. Sometimes I feel like a slab of meat thrown in a pressure cooker."

All the ladies looked at me.

"The pressurization changes on an airplane can cause bloating and gas especially if you've eaten something different from your normal menu that day. There's a Cuban restaurant in the Miami airport that has the best rice and beans. It's made with black beans, which have the reputation of being the most potent of the bean family. If you think eating beans then getting on an airplane won't wreak havoc on your system then you're sadly mistaken. I saw a pilot the other day order the rice and beans with a huge pile of raw onions on top. I was joking with him and told him I felt sorry for the other pilot who was going to be locked in the cockpit with him. He knew exactly what I was talking about, and he said that was what the extra oxygen mask was for! I told him that the co-pilot was going to need a heavy-duty gas mask!

"Also, sinuses can go ballistic and my eyes often become so bloodshot from the low humidity and exhaustion. It's not a good idea to fly with sinus problems or a cold either. Pressure changes affect everything on an airplane. My friend Denis, who's a pilot, told me his metal water bottle sprays out when he opens it. Also, everyone needs to be careful with yogurt containers and those little creamers for coffee. Aim them in the other direction, or at a passenger you don't like, when you open them on a plane."

"One time I opened my hand lotion and half the bottle squirted out like Old Faithful," Naomi said.

"Old Faithful, uh huh! Ha ha," said Pat.

Of course, the waiter came to the table again right in the middle of Naomi's lotion explosion demonstration and he gave us the 'what the hell are you women talking about now' look.

The group responded with a snort of dismissive laughter.

"OK ladies, maybe we should reel this conversation back in," said Pat.

I tried to change the subject, or at least get it back to a more practical consideration. "Have you ever seen what happens to a plastic water bottle upon descent? If it's been opened, the bottle distorts as it crunches inward, and can shrink to half its size." As I explained this, I demonstrated with my hands like a man crushing a beer can. "The galley has all kinds of loud popping and creaking noises during air pressure changes. It sounds like a weird science experiment."

Pat said, "I can't imagine what that does to a person's body."

"Yeah, any kind of body cavity can be affected." I laughed. "I'll tell you stories about farts some other time when we're not sitting at lunch."

The idea of farts drew a laugh from everyone.

Naomi said, "I hate being on an airplane with a screaming baby, but there's usually nothing you can do about it because their ears hurt. It's the same pressure changes you're talking about."

"You've got that right. By the time they're crying, it's too late. We have new parents flying out of Guatemala all the time with adopted babies. I try to let them know about keeping a small child constantly swallowing with a bottle or pacifier, especially during takeoff and landing."

"Lord, I've had a blocked ear on an airplane, and I thought my head was going to split wide open," Ethel said as she put both hands to her ears and pretended to scream.

I grimaced, thinking about the pain I suffered with all my own ear problems.

"I've already blown out my right eardrum on a flight. I have awful sinus problems so I know what it feels like."

"That's not a good omen for your job, is it?" Mary Ann said with concern, as she batted her heavily mascara-coated eyelashes.

"Yeah. It can be really scary. Every now and then, before landing, we'll see a passenger screaming in pain with their hands over their ears like Ethel just did. I'm usually the flight attendant standing in the middle of the aisle doing the hippopotamus yawns, instructing children and adults on how to relieve the pressure."

"I think I've tried about everything including chewing gum, but it doesn't work," said Ethel.

"That's because the real trick is to pull your jaw forward then down, as you yawn. I know I look like an idiot demonstrating how to yawn. But people don't understand until I literally stand in front of them with my mouth wide open; this usually helps unless your ear is already totally blocked. Then there's the Valsalva maneuver."

Just then the waiter came by to fill up the water glasses. Ethel had her hands over her ears, Naomi was pinching her nose and holding her breath like she was jumping into a swimming pool and I was doing hippopotamus yawns. He looked at us as though we were all crazy.

Naomi said, "I know all about that Val-whatever-thing-a-ma-jigger, pinching the nose closed and blowing. Supposed to equalize the pressure, unless you already have a cold. My boys always had something going on so it never worked for us, but I know it does for other people."

"I know how they feel; about thirty minutes before landing my ears start popping. I can tell when we've started descending even before any bells or announcements."

Since everybody seemed interested in this conversation about medical maladies, I went on, "I once saw a man who had what looked like a tumor about the size of a baseball on the top of his wrist. It blew up like a balloon during my flight! We found out he'd had blood drawn from the vein earlier that day. Our purser called for a doctor on board. Wouldn't ya know, there wasn't a doctor on that flight, but we did have a paramedic."

Pat set her coffee cup down. "What'd he have, some kind of a blood clot at the needle site?"

"That's exactly what the paramedic said. He told us to ice it down to try to control any further swelling, and then pray we didn't have to make an emergency landing. When we landed the man walked off the flight with the medics. I thought he was on his deathbed, but my friend Noelle, who knows more about medical stuff than I do, said the swelling probably went down after he got away from the pressurization on the plane."

Willa looked serious. "Wow. No doctor on board. You've always had such a weak stomach. Didn't you pass out when they took blood out of your dog?"

"Thanks for reminding me."

"What would you've done if it had ruptured?" Willa asked.

"Eww. I don't know. I'm just so glad whatever it was didn't explode. You know I'm not a very good blood-and-guts person. I've heard of three different incidents of sinus cavities exploding. Any time there is non-stop bleeding, we have to divert to the nearest airport immediately."

"And Pat," said Ethel, "watch out for that deep vein thrombosis on your flight to Europe, too. I've read a lot about it lately, especially with people our age."

"Oh yeah." Ethel had reminded me of something important, since this whole conversation came about because of Pat's upcoming travels.

"Pat, on your trip, be sure to get up and walk around every couple of hours on the plane. At least try to stand up and move your legs or do ankle circles. But keep in mind you didn't hear this from me. Technically, you're supposed to be in your seat."

"Thanks for the suggestion. I'll make a point to move around a lot. A friend of mine had a blood clot from exactly what we're talking about."

Pat, along with all of these ladies, knew a lot more than I did about medical problems, either from their own experiences or from friends.

"Y'all are reminding me of one of the worst flights I ever encountered as a new hire. Looking back, it's funny, but it definitely wasn't at the time. We had a layover in Chicago, and when we arrived at the airport the next morning, crew schedule informed us we'd been reassigned. Instead of going home, they'd added another day onto our trip with a flight to Rochester, Minnesota."

"Isn't that when you missed your friend Susan's wedding?" Willa asked.

I nodded.

"Yeah, reassignments are a way of life for a flight attendant, especially on holidays or when I have big plans. Being reassigned was bad enough, but missing the wedding just about killed me."

"I felt so bad for you when you missed our Christmas gathering last year at Andrea's house too," said Willa.

"Yeah, you're right, but that was because of a random drug test that just happened to be on Christmas Eve. The drug test person was late and made me too late to drive to New Jersey so I went home to your empty house. I was not a happy camper for my first Christmas up here.

"Anyway Willa, let me get back to my story. So, when I finally calmed down about the reassignment to Rochester, and got back into work mode, a light bulb went off in my head: Oh no! The Mayo Clinic is there."

The Mayo Clinic is one of the premier medical facilities in the USA and the world.

"One of the worst things that can happen on a flight is a medical emergency. Those flights to Rochester are full of Mayo Clinic patients. Any one of them is a ticking time bomb for a medical crisis, which would require diverting the airplane. Usually, we have at least one senior flight attendant on board who's handled many medical situations before, but not on this trip. Twenty or thirty year veterans avoided this trip, making me the most senior, with three months of experience.

"Recognizing the Mayo Clinic destination, I told all my fellow newbie crew members to be prepared: mentally review what they had learned about the oxygen tanks with different flow rates, CPR, heart attacks, and any other medical situation. Get ready. We could see a variety of medical problems coming on this one flight.

"Of course, the other three flight attendants looked at me like I was crazy until the agent working the flight told us to be prepared for thirty wheelchair passengers coming on. A typical flight might have only one or two. This flight also had people on oxygen. Boarding began, and every person wanted a pillow and blanket, though we only had a few available. Then we had to do a water service before we even took off because everyone had to take his or her pills.

"After a frenzied workout getting everyone situated, I was just waiting for something to happen, when an elderly, extremely thin, white-haired man rang his call button. I took one look at his pale-gray face and thought for sure he was having a heart attack. I asked the other flight attendant if she'd turned on his oxygen because he didn't look so good. She said she had, so I went to him prepared for the worst. Luckily, he only wanted a pillow!

"In the middle of the flight a huge group of them started comparing their medical conditions. It was like an Olympic sport. Whoever had the most or the worst medical conditions won the Gold. One person next to the window was yelling about his gall bladder and liver problems, someone else yelled out about their quadruple-zillion bypass surgeries, but 'bionic woman' won the prize. Every time someone yelled out about his or her particular ailment, she'd already had it. I thought for sure we'd have to use our medical training, but thank heavens, it proved to be an uneventful trip. All these patients made it to their destination without any trauma."

Naomi said, as if she commiserated with my passengers, "That's what old people do, complain about their ailments."

I didn't know if she was just making a comment or whether she really didn't consider herself in the same category.

I gave Pat a last bit of advice.

"Drink a lot of water so you won't feel like you're in a pressure cooker. The humidity on a plane is only three percent, so you dehydrate fast. Take a bottle of water with you to your seat. Drink lots of fluids, but avoid coffee, tea, and alcohol, which are all dehydrating. You know alcohol affects you more on a plane."

"I know all about the alcohol at high altitudes," Pat said. "I've seen what happens to some people."

"Reminds me of the time I was working a trip to San Juan. This man drank just one little glass of wine. I happened to be walking by and couldn't help notice his expressionless eyes and his face was as gray as a battleship.

"I stopped and asked his wife if he was okay. In a strange robot-like voice, she told me he wasn't feeling well.

"By now, I'm thinking, why didn't she ring the call button? It's not called 'the heart attack button' for no reason. Her husband looked really, really bad.

"Then she said, with her teeth clinched together, 'We'd better not miss our cruise.'

"I gently touched the man's arm and asked him if he was having trouble breathing. He nodded and whispered that he had a heart condition.

"That put us into emergency medical mode. I stayed with him while another flight attendant brought an oxygen canister and someone else called for a doctor on board. This time there were two doctors, and one was a cardiologist. He asked the wife if her husband was on any medications. She reached in her bag and pulled out a printout that nearly hit the floor. Her husband was on every drug imaginable, but didn't have any of them handy. They'd packed all the medicines in their checked luggage.

"We put him on oxygen. Then the doctor asked around if anyone had an extra nitroglycerin pill. Fortunately, they were traveling with an AARP (American Association of Retired Persons) group. About twenty different people raised their hands and offered their supply of the heart attack drug.

"The purser asked the wife if she wanted an ambulance to meet the flight. The wife looked at her barely conscious husband and repeated, 'We better not miss our cruise just because you had to have a glass of wine.'

"I told her as delicately as possible that they most likely would be catching up with the cruise ship at the next port. He really didn't look very well and I heard the cardiologist prescribe hospitalization. She must have agreed to it, because the medics met the flight.

"The last moment before he was taken off the plane I heard her say, "I told you not to have a glass of wine, but do you listen to me? Nooo.""

The lunch ladies couldn't believe it. Naomi said, "What was wrong with that lady?"

"I don't know but Willa's daughter, Carolyn, told me about a lady in your neighborhood who was on a cruise when her husband died.

"Oh no! That's awful." A couple of the ladies said in unison.

"Actually the wife said it was no problem at all. If someone dies they just keep them in the refrigerator until the end of the cruise.

"Oh and that's nothing! Crazy spouses come out of the woodwork when traveling. My friend, Cherry, was working a flight back to the United States and right after takeoff a lady went into labor. The baby was coming fast. The woman was screaming in a foreign language and do you know what the husband did? When the flight attendants got to her, the husband was holding her legs together."

A collective gasp from the table.

Willa said, "Crazy fool. Was he going to hold her legs together for eight hours?"

"He wanted to make it to the U.S. for his anchor baby to be born so it would have citizenship in the U.S.A," said Pat.

Ethel asked, "What's an anchor baby?"

Pat explained. "It's a child born in the U.S. to foreign national parents. It improves the chances of securing eventual citizenship for themselves."

Pat said this matter-of-factly, giving us all an insight into how she must have grilled witnesses on the stand in her good old days as a defense attorney.

"Haven't you heard about the maternity tourism industry here in the U.S.?" Willa asked.

"Well, their little ploy didn't work that time, because the plane turned right around and went back."

The waiter came to clear the table, and as a courtesy to help him out, I handed him my plate, then thanked him for a job well done. He looked stunned, then smiled like I had just made his day. *It's amazing how a few words of kindness can go a long way.*

That proved to be enough medical talk for one lunch.

As we all dispersed, I said, "Be healthy, and Pat, have a great trip."

On the way home I said to Willa, "I'm glad you don't talk about health problems all the time."

"Oh pshaw! I've got better things to talk about."

"Willa! I haven't heard that expression in a million years. Where did that come from? Do I bring out that little bit of the southern you still have left in you? I'd swear the Alabama girl just came out, even after forty-five years of Long Island living."

My mama used to say, "Oh pshaw! Just do it." I guess this was the southern version of Nike's slogan. My mama was way ahead of her time.

LONDON BOMBING BRIEFING

As all the crew boarded the airplane for our trip to London, Carl, the purser, told us to stow our luggage as quickly as possible and come back up to first class for a briefing with the captain.

I recognized the captain when he came out of the cockpit, holding a handful of paperwork. "Hey Mike, didn't we fly together a couple of months ago? Another flight from New York to London, you know, during the IRA (Irish Republican Army) bombings in England and Ireland."

He looked at me, feigning a faint glint of recognition.

"Yeah, we've flown together before. I'm sure we have."

Usually I can't recall who was on my last trip three days ago, but I specifically remembered him and the flight.

"Weren't you the captain when we had the bombing briefing?"

"Oh yeah. Were you on that flight?" Now he remembered. Maybe not me in particular, but he knew exactly which trip I was referring to. It clearly brought back memories.

"Yes, I was."

He then told the others about that day.

"You know we have to be prepared for anything, especially if it's already a news event. The runway at Heathrow airport was hit by two of five mortar bombs launched by the IRA, with threats of further attacks."

I added what I remembered.

"Yeah, and you told us if there was any aggression toward our airplane upon landing or taxiing in, we'd make every effort to keep the aircraft moving out of range of any bombs." I looked around at my fellow crew members then at the captain. "No offense, but that wasn't very reassuring to hear."

"Wow. That's scary," said one of the crew.

One of the female flight attendants asked, "Did you get bombed?"

"No, thank heavens. We landed safely. Taxied in as usual. But I can tell you; sitting on my jump seat was nerve-wracking. We were prepared for anything to happen during that landing."

Carl said, "Well, I hope our trip today goes as usual with standard procedures. Bombing briefings—that's the first time I've heard of that one."

Another crew member said, "Just another typical day on the job."

The captain filled us in on weather, arrival time, and any other issues that could affect the flight. With our routine briefing over, we all dispersed to take our positions on the plane for boarding. I was working business class on this trip. After the meal service we usually ask the passengers to lower their window shades, not only to make it easier to see the movies on the overhead monitors but also to block the light coming in at sunrise. When the sun comes up in the morning on an overnight flight, it's like a painful spotlight in the eyes of the passengers waking up from a sound sleep.

A businessman, still in his suit coat and tie, not only refused to pull down the window shade next to his seat but also was adamant about no one touching it. After he fell asleep, I went over and closed his shade, thinking that earlier he had just wanted to look out the window into the darkness, for whatever reason,

After the completion of the meal services in all cabins, we're allowed to take a break. I made my way to the back galley, and on the way I used a coat hanger to lean over sleeping people to lower the few window shades that were still up. During our breaks, the favorite pastime has always been galley gossip and telling jokes. Some of the flight attendants had gathered in the back galley, and when I got to the group, I told them about the business class passenger who went berserk over his window shade.

"What was that all about?" said Linda, the galley flight attendant, as she emptied out some soda inserts, and cleaned up the area. "You did close that shade, didn't you?"

"Yeah I did, but I don't have the slightest idea what his problem is." I shrugged, and propped up an empty soda insert on the floor. Since there's nowhere for us to sit, we perch on the hard plastic drink can inserts, which are approximately the same size as a twenty-four can case of beer. It provides us with a place to rest for two minutes.

No sooner had a rather thin flight attendant sat down on top of an insert, when we hit turbulence. Her insert flipped and she ended up sitting on the floor with her tushy inside the plastic box. Stuck. It took three of us to get her out, two to pull her up from the front and one to pull the insert from behind.

She popped out and said, "Oh boy! It's going to be fun explaining these bruises to my husband."

"If you have to go to the doctor, they're going to think you've been abused," I said. "Be careful, because recently my cousin Ellen was riding horses when one of the riders was thrown off. Ellen took her friend to the hospital just to make sure there weren't any broken bones, and the nurses handed her all these pamphlets about domestic violence for abused women. Ellen laughed and told those nurses, 'Yeah, her abuser weighs two thousand pounds.'"

Another flight attendant walked up, joining our group. "I just had another passenger try to order a drink using their call button. They were yelling into it just as I walked by, 'Where's my Coke? I ordered it a while ago.'"

Linda said, "Did you ask them if they wanted fries with that order?"

Another flight attendant came to the back to retrieve a handful of paper towels from the lav.

"I just had a passenger reach for a drink and drop it on the computer of the man sitting next to her."

"Whoa, I bet he's mad!" I said.

"Yeah, he's not a happy camper. Of course, you know there are two types of flight attendants, those that have spilled a drink on a laptop, and those that haven't spilled on a laptop *yet*. I feel really bad about his computer but at least I didn't do it *this* time."

She took off up the aisle and I said, "Sounds like what happened to me on a recent trip. I was standing in front of first class on a DC10 when a passenger asked for champagne. I know how to open a bottle of champagne, but I hadn't checked to see if it was cold. You know about opening a warm bottle, it explodes - shooting out the cork and spraying champagne out like a fire hose. I'd never seen a cork go that far! It pinged off the back wall of first class; passengers were dodging it like a bullet. I got soaked from head to toe, and worked the rest of the day smelling like a brewery. What a mess. But the passengers enjoyed the show. One of 'em even clapped. I'm just glad no one had a laptop open at the time."

A junior flight attendant, with a heavy Texas drawl, waved her hand to the group to get everyone's attention.

"Let me tell y'all something. Boy howdy, you gotta hear this one. On my last trip, coming back from Cancun, a huge tour group came on. They'd been partying together on the beach all week, and in order to board the plane, they had to put on a minimum of clothes: flip-flops, shorts, and tank tops.

"When the purser announced for us to prepare for landing, I went through doing compliance checks, telling people to stow their belongings. When I turned around to the next person I just about died. The young man seated in 26A had fallen asleep with his leg propped up on the seat in front of him. And dern if his jewels weren't hanging out of his shorts."

"Jewels? Jewels? You don't mean...his...?" said one flight attendant, overhearing this story, as she inhaled audibly and put her hand over her mouth to hide her giggle.

"Yes, ma'am," Ms. Texas said, drawn out as slow-as-molasses. "Dang, I didn't know what to do, so I sang out to one of the senior flight attendants in the back galley for some help.

"I guess she could see the hanging gardens of Babylon from way back there 'cause that senior mama didn't hesitate. She took one look up the aisle, took the whole situation in quicker than a blivit, and flew toward that fella like a goose after a June bug. She filled his ears with a few choice words to wake him up, then she leaned in close, pointed her finger right at his nose and snapped her words off like machine gun bullets. 'Put your tray table up. Pull your seat back forward. And...stow... your... *dick*.' "

"No, she didn't," everybody said at the same time. One girl laughed so hard she snorted like a donkey. That started us all laughing.

The whole time we had been talking in the galley, Linda had been fidgeting with her acrylic fake fingernails.

She had a broken one, so she turned to the rest of us and asked, "Does anyone have any superglue?"

As new hires, we were required to keep our fingernails painted, in addition to keeping our hair cut to a certain length. She tried to fix the nail, not only because it was aggravating, but also because her job depended on passing the grooming checks during the first nine months of probation.

Another crew member pulled out a tube of superglue from her tote bag and handed it over with the warning, "Now be careful."

Linda went to the back of the galley where she diligently tried to fix her expensive broken nail.

The next thing we heard was, "Oh crap! Uh oh! Uh oh! Help!"

With the bumping around on the airplane, she had glued her fingers together!

"Quick! Pull 'em apart!" someone said.

Too late.

"Tell me she didn't just do that. How do you get 'em apart?" I didn't have the slightest idea because I've never had fake fingernails.

Another person sporting long nails said, "She's not going to get 'em apart until she gets to the hotel where she can soak her fingers in nail polish remover. None of the passengers will have any either because it would've been confiscated in TSA. "

"You gotta be kidding! That's hours from now." This exclamation came from the superglue victim. "What am I going to do?"

All she could do was laugh at how silly she looked as she held up her right hand with the thumb and middle two fingers stuck together. Her pinky finger stuck out like she was drinking from a teacup. "Does this look stupid or what? And I'm on an airplane… what am I going to do?"

"Well, you do look prissy but it could've been worse. On one of my other flights, I saw a flight attendant rip her fingernail off. She got it caught in the accordion-fold door on a DC10 storage closet."

"You mean a fake fingernail. Right?" Linda grimaced while holding up her prissy fingers.

"No, a real fingernail. It was the most gruesome thing I've ever seen."

"Oh no…on a plane! Then she's stuck there for hours, in pain and bleeding before she can get to a doctor." Linda grimaced.

"Yeah. That's the worst part. And I know of two flight attendants who knocked out their front teeth. One of them was a friend of mine. He was trying to open a metal door that was stuck on the front of a beverage cart. He bent over to put all his force into his pull. And of course, it came flying open and knocked out his front teeth."

Everybody said, "Eww," at the same time.

Then one of the crew said, "We'd better figure out how to do this service without the galley person. Who wants to take over setting up and cooking the meals?"

"Some people will do anything to get out of work," I said, halfway serious. We were all thinking about how this freak accident had created a lot of problems, not only for her, but also for all of us working this trip.

Someone else said, "Maybe she could make shadow puppets on the wall?" That started us making jokes and laughing because Linda looked so pitiful.

Needless to say, *Superglue Girl* was out of commission for the rest of that flight. She couldn't lift a twenty-pound soda insert with one hand or push a three hundred-pound cart one-handed or even pour a glass of water. Now we had to gear up for the coach breakfast service. All the flight attendants, including me, pitched in to cover for her. Pushing the carts down the aisle, we tried to stay calm and professional. Then we would hear that flight attendant's snort, and we'd all start laughing all over again. It took us longer than usual to finish the service, but we had fun. Her laughing was contagious and the passengers joined in too.

As soon as I'd finished helping with the breakfast service in coach, I headed back up to business class to get ready for that breakfast service. As we started the service, window-shade businessman woke up. He started ringing his call button like he was having a heart attack. I went to him and found the man hyperventilating that someone had touched his shade. Somehow, he thought this could break the seal on the window and crash the plane. He had hidden his fear of flying from us, and I patiently explained the non-technical workings of a window shade and the safety features of the double layers of glass in the window.

Being facetious, what I really wanted to say to him was, "In my whole career, I've never seen anyone sucked out of an airplane window. But there's always a first time."

WHO IS THIS MAN? A STALKER?

Returning from my London trip, I had just pulled into Willa's driveway and parked. While dragging my luggage from the rear of my hatchback, I heard someone behind me and turned around to find a middle-aged man wearing shorts and a polo shirt, walking toward me.

"Hello," I challenged him with my newly acquired New York attitude.

I was proud of myself, that hello came out like 'what do you want buster?' rather than my typical friendly greeting from growing up in the South.

This stranger kept on barreling toward me. *Just because I'm wearing a skirt doesn't mean I'm not dangerous with my 'killer' high-heeled shoes on. Although frankly, all they're killing right now are my feet.*

He stopped only a few feet away and said, "Hey Elizabeth, I heard you almost killed a passenger?"

"What?"

Ignoring the look on my face, which I know was part bewilderment but mostly suspicion, he went on with his grilling.

"Was Willie Mays really on your flight? Is the sand really pink in Bermuda? Did you really break up with that baseball player? How did you do out in Steamboat last week with the airline ski team?"

I gave him the stink-eye. *How was he privileged to all this personal information about me? I don't have the slightest idea who this guy is.* Maybe he's …a stalker. Or maybe he was a spy from the airline. I should defend myself but I could get fired for killing a passenger.

Finally I squeezed in a "Pardon me?"

"Did you get Willie Mays's autograph? He was the greatest. Willa told me all about the passenger you had to get a wheelchair for, just to get him off the plane. What happened? I only heard part of the story. What did you do to him? Was it really your fault?"

"Uh. No, it wasn't. Well, it wasn't exactly my fault. Well, kind of, but I didn't mean to." Getting more and more frustrated with his questions, I asked, "Do I know you?"

"Oh. I'm sorry," he said as he put out his hand in a friendly manner. "I'm John. You know, the mailman. I've been the house sitter here," pointing to Willa's house, "for your aunt and uncle, for the last twenty-five years or so. Well, up until your uncle passed away. Bless his soul."

Uh oh. Willa, that explains a lot and he reads the addresses on my mail. I finally relaxed a little. "House sitting? They don't have any pets."

"Yeah, but somebody had to wind all those clocks and collect their mail when they went on trips."

"You've got to be kidding me," I said. "I will pay you *not* to wind all those damn clocks. There must be a hundred of 'em. Do you know how long it took me not to jump out of bed each time that big grandfather clock clanged out the hour? I thought it was my alarm clock."

"Yeah, that clock is really loud. So what happened with the passenger?"

"That passenger incident was not my fault. Did Willa tell you about it?"

"Not all of it."

"Well, let me back up and fill you in a bit. For the first six months of employment, we don't have flight privileges. Basically, we're all stuck at our initial base. We're not able to return home to see friends and family. I really don't know how people deal with leaving their children for that long. It's difficult enough to handle necessities, like banking, checking mail, and whatever else may arise in the meantime, or to retrieve more clothes. Some new hires were shipped directly to base from training. Similar to Monopoly: go directly to jail or in our case—our base; don't go home to collect any essentials that you may need.

"Many flight attendants were still living out of the single suitcase they had originally brought from home when they left for training six weeks earlier. When they arrived in New York they had to go out to buy sweaters and coats for the cold weather.

"There was one little bit of hope for us newbies, though; the airline did a test period of providing frequent flyer passengers with travel vouchers for flight passes. These vouchers could be given as a reward to airline employees who were helpful or did something special. If we received three of these travel vouchers we could trade them in for a free airline ticket. It was a win-win situation for everyone because we worked hard to make the passengers happy in return for these vouchers. It's the only way we could fly home without paying for a full fare ticket.

"I'd just learned how to make a drink called a B-52 and fixed one for an appreciative passenger who immediately gave me a free travel-pass voucher. I thought, wow, B-52s work great. Now I know how to get more of the free travel passes. On the very next leg, a first class passenger came on board dressed in a suit and tie, and asked if I knew how to make any specialty cocktails.

"I got excited, thinking he might give me another pass ticket in return, so I told him I could make a B-52. I proceeded to mix a mini-bottle each of Grand Marnier, Baileys, and Kahlua, the equivalent of four-and-a-half shot glasses in one drink."

"Hmm," John said, "that's a lot of alcohol."

"Yeah, and he drank it, fast. Then he asked for another one. I'd created a monster and didn't know how to handle it. To stall for time, I explained I'd have to wait until we got up in the air to make him another drink. When we started our in-flight service, he drank another B-52 just as fast as the first, and wanted a third. My co-worker, Jake, was a senior flight attendant so I asked his advice. 'How am I going to cut off the lush in 4B? He's drinking too much, way too fast.'

"Jake turned around to check him out and asked, 'You don't mean that dishrag, do ya?'

"A quick glance in 4B's direction explained Jake's comment. Mr. Lush had passed out with his body draped across the seat like a wet noodle. 'Holy Moly! Is he dead?' If he hadn't been strapped in his seatbelt, he would've slid right out of the seat. I realized at that point he must have taken quite a few nips before the flight. Maybe his drinking to excess would've been understandable at a younger, foolish, inexperienced age.

Back in my college days, if a guy passed out from drinking too much, we would paint his fingernails bright red just to illustrate how lame-brained and senseless it was to drink that much. It would've been fun to do that here, but clearly inappropriate, and I hadn't the slightest idea what the protocol was on an airplane. Now he was my problem.

"In desperation, I asked his business associate, seated next to Mr. 4B, 'Does he have to drive anywhere after landing?'

"I could tell he was totally disgusted with the whole situation. He grimaced and said, 'No, but we have a business meeting an hour after we land.'"

At this point in my story, John the mailman jumped in with what he'd heard from Willa. "You had to get a wheelchair to get his dead-drunk carcass off the plane. Wow. Some people." He was shaking his head. "What about Willie Mays?"

"Don't even mention him in the same breath with that problem passenger. Willie Mays was sooo nice. I wasn't going to bother him. Just as I walked up the aisle he stretched his big right arm out in front of me, and I teased, 'Don't you hit me with that powerful arm.' He laughed, and I asked him where he was playing golf."

"Golf? Willie Mays? You said golf?" John asked, perplexed, "But he's a world famous baseball player."

"I know, but he was so excited to talk about anything other than baseball. As a matter of fact, he told me that he was on his way to Palm Springs to play a round with his buddies. He allowed some of the small boys from coach to come up to get his autograph. They were so excited to meet a legend. He was such a gracious man."

For a mailman, John seemed to be in no hurry. "I like to hear nice stories about famous people." I nodded in agreement and started edging toward the front door to give him the hint that I was tired and ready to collapse. As I was walking up the front steps it hit me. How did John know I broke up with the baseball player? I hadn't told Willa anything about that.

SUBWAY DANGERS

That weekend, Willa's nineteen year old granddaughter, Jeanne, came to visit. A marathon runner, she was full of energy, and usually sported her dark-brown hair in a bouncing ponytail. Jeanne also loved vintage clothing, thus closet diving at Willa's house always produced some interesting finds that had come full circle in fashion trends, and were back in style now.

For me, the cache upstairs had a particular allure as it allowed me to take a step back in time. Jeanne and I enthusiastically rummaged through the antique collection of prom dresses, hats, shoes, sequined cocktail dresses, and other leftover clothing from Willa's three daughters that continued to grace the biggest cedar-lined walk-in closets I've ever seen.

One of the first things Jeanne wanted to do was see New York City. I jumped at the chance to show her around since I considered myself a seasoned tour guide after living on Long Island for a year.

Willa gave us grandmotherly over-cautious advice. "Keep your purse in front of you, and watch your surroundings at all times." Then we got the index finger lecture pointed at each of us. "And don't talk to strangers."

"Yes ma'am." We nodded our heads like little kids, mainly just to pacify her fears.

"I heard a story about men on the subway who will cut your fingers off to get your rings. So don't wear any jewelry. Are you listening to me? Be careful!"

We both totally ignored this gruesome anecdote, thinking it too preposterous.

Jeanne and I found two seats together on the L.I.R.R. (Long Island Rail Road) train from Manhasset into the city. While the outside world whizzed by the windows, we hunkered down over our maps, trying to decide whether to start with sightseeing, or go shopping, or go to Canal Street in Chinatown. When we arrived at Penn Station, we followed the blue overhead signs for the 'E' subway. As we headed toward the steps everyone started running.

"Quick! Run! I hear it coming," I yelled at Jeanne, as if I knew what I was doing.

I just followed the lead of the people who did this as a daily routine. Everyone started running when they heard the loud rumblings of the subway pulling in to the stop, because no one wanted to wait for the next one in the heat and stench of the underground tunnels.

"Whew, that was close. We barely made it," I said as we slid into two seats.

"Now we're almost there; shop 'til we drop."

At the next subway stop, the doors opened, and in walked a muscular man carrying an enormous set of industrial bolt cutters. He casually dangled the tool by one of the three-foot long handles, but what caught my eye was the saucer-sized cutter head. The razor sharp, steel blades sparkled as he took a seat right across from us.

He was wearing a tank top, shorts, and tennis shoes. He had no tool belt, nothing that gave us any impression that he needed this over-sized 'finger-cutter' for any type of work.

Jeanne and I both bolted upright in our seats; trying to be discrete, we cut our eyes at each other. Without saying a word, we knew we were both thinking the same thing: Was this guy going to cut our fingers off?

Here we were, in broad daylight, in the middle of summer on a not-so-crowded subway. I kept an eye on him, as he checked out his surroundings with an intense stare, stopping his gaze on each person, scoping out his next victim.

While trying to stay calm and not look alarmed, I said under my breath, "We're getting off at the next stop," even though this was not anywhere near our intended destination.

When the subway opened, we jumped up and made a run for it, thinking we were finally safe. Damned if he didn't get off too. He bolted out the other door at the same time. He turned, glaring straight at us.

Jeanne and I looked at each other, wide-eyed.

We both yelled, "Run!" as we ran like hell back into the subway car just as the door closed behind us. We made it—without him.

SAINT MARTIN
AND LESSONS LEARNED
FROM FELLOW TRAVELERS

I walked into the kitchen carrying a four-pound ball of Gouda cheese.

Aunt Willa looked at it and shook her head. "I told you not to bring home any more of those 'bowling balls.' There's only the two of us here." This was her reference to the huge balls of cheese that I brought back from my trips to Saint Martin.

This Dutch cheese is sold everywhere, including the airport, because the southern half of the island is part of the Netherlands.

There are four different names for this island. Sint Maarten or St. Maarten is Dutch and is flanked to the north by Saint Martin or St. Martin, which is French. In English, this northeastern Caribbean island is called Saint Martin. Can that be any more confusing?

The Dutch are world renowned for their cheese, and St. Maarten is a popular place for casinos and nightlife. The French Saint Martin is a popular nude beach destination and noted for its French cuisine.

As a vacation destination St. Martin's beaches were often compared to those of other islands. After one of my flights to St. Martin, two pilots, a captain and a first officer, were in the van going to the hotel, arguing about which was a better place to vacation, Aruba or St. Martin.

The captain said, "St. Martin has gorgeous beaches and really great discounts on jewelry and watches."

The first officer countered with, "But it never rains in Aruba. The weather's not going to mess up your vacation. And think about it, in St. Martin, if you take a wife or girlfriend, the shopping could cost you a lot."

After thinking about it for a second the captain conceded, and said, "Yeah. You're right."

They each had good points; both obviously had their favorite spots for vacation memories. Each island has its own distinctive qualities: Saint Martin with its split personality and Aruba with its dry climate.

But where do you go for fence surfing? Saint Martin, of course. You've probably heard of wave surfing, wind surfing, and kite surfing? So why not surf in the jet blast of an airplane? You're probably thinking what idiot would do that? Maho Beach is a place where you can get up close and personal with the jet blast from jumbo airplanes.

There's a sign posted at the site:

Dangerous jet blast from departing and incoming aircraft can cause severe physical harm resulting in extreme bodily harm and/or death.

It includes a picture of a person tumbling across the gravel because of jet blast. The sign actually spurs the enthusiasm of those who have been partying on the beach all day. Without the warning it wouldn't be nearly as exciting.

As the airplanes turn to takeoff, their jet engines rev up to full throttle. Thrill-seekers line up, holding onto the top rail of the fence just behind the blast of the screaming engines, for the superman ride of their life—that is, if they can hang on. The ones that get blown off go tumbling across the gravel and rocks, adding an enticing element of danger.

I think there's a competition among the pilots to try to knock the fence surfers off. Most of them won't admit it, except my pilot friend Ron. He likes to add to the entertainment by gunning the engine an extra notch.

Watching airplanes land from this beach is also a popular attraction. Runway 10 is so short that airplanes descend directly over the beach about twenty feet above onlooker's heads. It's so popular a place for airplane enthusiasts that local bars and restaurants post the airline schedules. The Sunset Beach Bar even broadcasts the radio transmissions between the pilots and the control tower.

One of my flight attendant friends, Peggy, is also from Raleigh. We arranged to work a Saint Martin trip together. Peggy, six months junior to me with the airline, had never been to Saint Martin, so we were talking about the various things we could do there.

Another flight attendant suggested, "Why don't you go check out the nude beach? It's only about fifteen minutes from our layover hotel."

Not having decided on any other excursion, Peggy and I went out exploring. We took off walking in the direction of the nude beach after deciding it might be something fun to talk about, and if we didn't make it there, that would be fine too; at least we would get some fresh air.

North Carolina is not known for nude beaches. At one of the coastal towns, there was a political meeting about whether to allow nudity on a particular beach. Someone suggested issuing permits. What is the nudist going to do with a permit, attach it to their 'bumper'? I can just picture the beachgoers in Saint Martin wearing bumper stickers.

A few years ago in the eastern part of the state, a group bought an old tobacco farm, to turn into a nudist colony. Well, this was a big to-do in our neck of the woods. A television news reporter went out to interview the neighbors to find out what they thought about this curious situation.

Just next door to the property in question, they found a little, gray-haired lady out picking green beans in her garden. She was wearing a long-sleeved, flowered dress and a wide-brimmed straw hat. The reporter was quite pleased with himself, discovering such a colorful, old-fashioned neighbor close by. He thought for sure she would be very upset and it would make a great story.

The over-zealous reporter approached her, followed by a big TV camera and microphone, and started the interview excitedly with, "What do you think about a nudist colony moving in next door to you?"

This wise old lady didn't blink an eye. "Them chiggers are gonna' eat 'em up," she said, referring to an insect that burrows under the skin causing a nasty welt that itches much worse than a mosquito bite. They go for exposed skin.

Peggy and I were still making our way, on our adventure, toward the nude beach, which everyone had assured us was only fifteen minutes away. We didn't bring any suntan lotion, thinking we would only be gone for a little while. I thought for sure we would get sidetracked with shopping or stopping for a bite to eat. No such luck. The deserted road to the beach just got hotter, and we became sweatier in the broiling sun. Forty-five minutes into this trek, we passed some people coming from the opposite direction. They told us to keep going just around the bend, to the left. We trudged on for a few more minutes and made it to the ultimate objective of our 'educational' expedition. We followed a well-worn path to a scenic over-look on a cliff above the beach. It felt strange to think of the many people who had been there before us. At least we weren't the only voyeurs around. Or did that make it worse? The beach was covered with a sundry of sizes, shapes and ages of people, and in my opinion a large majority of them should not have taken their clothes off.

Of course, every nude beach has a "manly" man, who struts around showing off. On this beach, this distinction belonged to a well-endowed man who had his long blond hair pulled back into a ponytail. He was obviously enjoying the attention he was attracting.

It didn't take us long to quench our curiosity and start heading back toward the hotel.

By the time we returned, we were so sunburned. We had gotten absolutely fried. The next day on the plane our fellow crew members joked with us about which of our body parts were sunburned. Some of the guys even said that if we needed any help putting on lotion, they would gladly oblige. They were just teasing—kind of.

Guess who showed up on our plane the next day? Mr. Manly Man. I went to find Peggy, to tell her the man from the nude beach was there and to see if she would recognize him with his clothes on.

She looked the man up and down, (mostly down) and then asked me, "How can you tell he's the one from the beach?" I could see she thought I had x-ray vision.

"Jeez, Peggy. He's the one with the pony tail."

My friend Meg told me about her experience on a vacation to Saint Martin. She and her husband Bert, along with several of their friends, stayed on the French side. While their hotel was not located directly on a nude beach, it was next to a topless area and further down was one of the clothes discretionary nude beaches.

After a few hours of drinking and partying, Meg and Bert, along with two other couples, decided to wander down to the nude beach. On this gorgeous Caribbean beach, they decided to join in (*when in Rome*), stripped down, and went into the ocean. They returned to find someone had made off with all of their possessions: their towels, room keys, car keys, and clothes. Everything was gone. If this was a joke by some of the others in their group, it wasn't funny.

Not only were they embarrassed, devastated, and angry, but also worse still, they had to get back to their hotel—sans clothes. Hiding in the bushes and behind parked cars, the middle-aged group skulked back. Meg, the smallest in the group, was elected to sneak up to her hotel room and retrieve anything that would cover the other five naked people, whom she left hiding in the bushes. Fortunately, Meg and Bert left a room key hidden in a secret spot, just in case one of them wanted to return early. And boy, were they glad they did. Meg, clad only in two big tropical leaves taken out of someone's landscape, made her way across the parking lot and up to the second floor.

She told me later, "I looked like someone in a scene out of a slap-stick comedy. I held up two huge tropical leaves, one covering my front and the other in the back, covering my butt. I could've been in a 007 movie. You should have seen me slinking through the hallways, hiding behind the maid's carts, and big potted plants. Then I peered around the corners to see if anyone was coming and took off running like a bat-out-of-hell to the next corner. Thank heavens I didn't run into anyone in the elevator, but I'm sure I flashed the surveillance cameras. Oh, what the hell"

When she made it to their room, she threw on some clothes and grabbed everything she could find. Towels, shirts and any piece of clothing that might fit, then went back down to rescue her patiently waiting naked husband and friends.

If someone had seen her, think of the vacation story they would have to tell!

What a tale! (No pun intended.)

This costly lesson provided me with sound advice: don't leave your valuables unattended. When Meg found out that no one else in their group knew anything about the prank, they called the police. All of the locks on their hotel room doors had to be replaced and one of the rental cars turned up stolen. What at first appeared to be an outrageous practical joke was nothing of the kind.

This advice was reinforced by the stories of other flight attendants. In the van going to the hotel, one girl told about her vacation catastrophe. They had rented a car and her family left all their valuables in the locked car and trunk, while they went to the beach. They came back to find someone had broken into the trunk and stolen everything. Luckily, she had left her wedding rings in the safe in the hotel.

Another pilot, sitting in the back of the van, related a scuba diving incident. He had just started swimming out and was still in shallow water when he spotted something shiny on the sandy bottom. He grabbed the object, which turned out to be a set of car keys, and tucked them into his pocket. When he got out of the water and took a closer look at what he had picked up, it turned out to be his own keys. Evidently, the keys had fallen out of his pocket right before he spotted them.

I told him, "You had a really good angel watching over you that day."

THE EXCITEMENT OF GOING
TO RIO AGAIN

Who doesn't want to go to Rio? My next flight turned out to be a lot more fun because I was a little more prepared to stay up all night than on my last trip, when I was called out on reserve with no sleep. Even so, my friend's son still refers to all-nighters as 'comatose trips' because that's what we feel like the day after.

My idea of Rio is New York City, New Orleans, and Miami's South Beach all rolled up into one—on steroids. Walking down the street in this city, with a population of over six million, gives me the same congested metropolitan feeling as walking down the streets of New York.

Flight attendants, as well as the passengers on the flights to Rio, talk about the magnet that draws many people to this city—its famous carnival celebration, the largest in the world. *Mardi Gras* in New Orleans is minor league compared to the non-stop, marathon partying for which the Brazilians are famous. This celebration reflects the heartbeat of the people. What appears to be frenzied excitement is actually the product of yearlong preparation in which participants, from all walks of life, scrimp and save every penny to create elaborate and expensive costumes for the parades.

They live for this; it keeps the pulse of the Brazilian spirit alive in these impoverished people as they prepare for carnival. I have heard that Brazilians, who are famous for the Samba and the Bossa Nova, don't stop dancing for days.

On the way to our layover hotel, we drove by world-renowned beaches, Copacabana and Ipanema. Miles of expansive, white-sand shorelines were covered in scantily clad bodies; but one doesn't mind the crowds because the 'people watching' is extraordinary. Remember the famous song about Brazil, 'The Girl from Ipanema?' The song celebrated the Brazilian high-spirited charisma.

Brazilian beaches are like the people, friendly and energetic. Anyone is welcome to play beach soccer with the locals by day or dance non-stop all night long at the clubs.

On Sunday, Oceanside Avenue is limited to pedestrian-only traffic and it's fun to watch this stretch known as a fashion runway. There are the weekend flea markets featuring arts and crafts created from the gemstones mined in Brazil. I've brought home everything imaginable made out of purple amethyst: wind chimes, coasters, art carvings, and, of course, jewelry.

And then there are Brazil's dazzling geodes, spherical-shaped, rocks. The ugly brown color on the outside hides a spectacular mass of crystals within, either clear quartz, or any array of colorful stones, such as amethyst.

Some of us were talking about going to the flea market when Jack, a pilot, said, "Y'all need to be careful. Let me tell you about my flea market adventure. I bought a fairly inexpensive, gorgeous geode, with brilliantly sparkling amethyst crystals inside. It was about the size of a tennis ball, and they wrapped it in tissue for me. I stuffed it in my pocket for the walk back to the hotel. On the way, a group of four teenage gang members held me up. I guess they spotted the large bulge in my pocket where usually a wallet or cash might be. I gladly relinquished my new purchase, handing over the wad of heavy tissue. They immediately took off running. And that's when I took off running in the other direction to get away before they realized they hadn't scored a bankroll. I was mighty glad that all they got was a rock."

I mentioned getting mugged rather casually but Rio is no different than any other large city. I learned to be street smart, not to wear jewelry, to stay in the crowds, and be aware of my surroundings. Someone once asked me if I was afraid of walking around in Rio.

I replied, "Are you kidding? I live in New York!"

CHRIST THE REDEEMER STATUE

While working this flight to Rio, several of us gathered in the galley to share suggestions for what to do on our layover. Marita had researched the travel guides and recommended we visit the famous Christ the Redeemer Statue, located on top of Corcovado Mountain.

Then another person said, "Oh yeah. I've seen that on the news. Anytime Rio is mentioned, it's the statue of Jesus, shown with outstretched arms overlooking the city."

After discussing the options, four of us eagerly decided to forgo sleep and take the tour. It sounded like a good idea, but by the time we got to the hotel, it was a different story. Most of the group had pooped out except for Marita and me. While we waited in the lobby for the tour to the top of Corcovado Mountain, Marita read from the brochure.

"Christ the Redeemer Statue is the largest Art Deco statue in the world. It's a hundred and thirty feet tall and ninety-eight feet across its wide-open arms and is one of the New Seven Wonders of the World."

The excursion included a ride up the steep slope of the mountain on a cog train. As the tram chugged the precipitous ascent overlooking the Tijuca rainforest, we looked out the window on this mostly cloudy day and could see only jungle overgrowth and more jungle overgrowth, and that was all I remembered. It might have been a scary ride except that we were both comatose from working all night and then going straight out on this tour. With the rocking motion of this rickety, old train, we both collapsed and slept right through until it stopped.

We stumbled out of the train at our destination. Standing there, trying to wake up, I stretched my neck out side-to-side, to recuperate from the awkward sleep position.

Just as I looked up I heard our tour guide announce, "Now you only have to climb two hundred and twenty steps to the viewing platform at the base of the statue."

In the middle of finger-combing my hair, I froze. "What? What did she just say?"

I looked straight up. "Oh shit."

Then I looked at Marita, as both of us just stood there, and contemplated the foreboding steps. We could read each other's minds through the red-roadmap in our bloodshot eyes.

"Okay, I'm here. I can do this. Just put one foot in front of the other. You can do it," I kept telling myself, as I pressed on, climbing up one step at a time, following Marita's footsteps.

"Don't think about it. Just imagine you're walking up steps to the ninth floor of an office building."

Marita offered this encouragement in a masochistic kind of way.

"Is that somehow supposed to make me feel better?" I asked, in between breaths. "I wish I'd done the Stairmaster more often...or at all."

Each step up presented a better view, so I stopped frequently and turned around under the pretense of taking a sightseeing break.

Oh wow! A magnificent 360° panoramic view of the city of Rio rewarded us when we finally reached the top. I was proud of myself and glad that I'd persevered. Conquering the climb allowed me to see why it was voted one of the Seven Wonders of the World.

In the last few years, the statue has been through major renovations. Elevators and escalators have been added to replace the exhausting ascent to the summit by foot. Now everyone, including the elderly, physically impaired or the just plain tuckered out, can join me in saying they enjoyed one of the most breathtaking sights in the world.

Before long, our tour leader appeared to round us up.

"You need to hurry, we need to start down."

"What? What did she say? No, she couldn't have just said that. We spent all this time and effort just to get up here. What's the rush?"

I didn't know about the changing weather patterns we were about to experience within the next few minutes.

Rapidly, the clouds moved in and engulfed us in the fog. As the visibility deteriorated, I stood there for a minute to take in this most fascinating phenomenon of standing in the clouds, and then realized that the statue was quickly vanishing and so were we. I'd always looked out the window of the airplane and wondered what a cloud felt like. Now I knew.

With our group leaving us behind, we scampered back down the steps at a much quicker pace than we had climbed up.

I had one more unexpected experience with the Christ statue later that night when we flew out of Rio. Having just taken off, the plane circled to gain altitude and the left wing lowered just as we cleared the clouds. Out of my window a spectacular, perfect view of the statue appeared in a mystical glowing light. From this close-up perspective it looked to me like the Redeemer Himself was standing on top of the clouds right outside my window.

The supernatural-looking figure stood in the night sky illuminated only from the spotlights shining from below. An awe-inspiring feeling came over me as I had a truly moving experience. Similar to those portraits where the eyes follow you around the room, I felt as if an omnipresent Christ Himself was looking straight at me. It made the hair stand up on the back of my neck and goosebumps ran up and down my arms.

I said my prayers.

"I promise to be a better person. I promise!"

And I'll even try to be nicer to the passengers.

POLTERGEIST IN THE KITCHEN

While driving home to Aunt Willa's house from a long trip, a flashback came to me of my first visit to Manhasset, Long Island. As an impressionable six-year-old, I'd endured my first airplane flight with no apparent desire or premonition for my future in air travel. Just getting off the airplane presented a challenge as I slid across the tarmac on the ice and snow.

Inside LaGuardia Airport, which looked exactly the same as it does today, my brother and I were overwhelmed by the loud noises and hustle of the frenzied people. Then the drive to Long Island appeared to be another world to us, wall-to-wall buildings and houses all covered in snow.

My mother, on the other hand, had lived in New York City previously. I never heard a lot about it, but it must have been quite exciting for her to leave a small town in Alabama to move to the Big Apple. The first time I saw Aunt Willa's house, I thought it was a castle, with the stonework and big metal spikes sticking out all around the base of the roof. I didn't know those spikes were actually snow guards that kept blocks of ice and snow from sliding off and taking the expensive slate shingles with it, or, worst case, killing someone. I just thought they looked menacing.

On that first visit, my cousins Andrea, Carolyn and Cindy, who were teenagers at the time, took my brother Mike and me into the City. When we came back home, I told Mama and Willa about having so much fun playing checkers with some nice men in the park.

I didn't think anything about it, but my mother, who was usually pretty easy going, whispered to Willa, "The homeless men. Oh good Lord. "

I guess these old memories popped into my head because Cindy, Aunt Willa's third daughter, had come home for a visit.

I dropped my bags inside the front door then headed toward the kitchen, where I heard voices. I walked in just as Cindy was rubbing her shin. "Uh oh. Did Jaws get you?"

"The dishwasher door fell down just as I was coming to greet you." She winced, still rubbing her leg.

"That's why we call it Jaws. Just when you least expect it, it attacks." I held my hand up like a claw. "You have to latch it closed, or it will get you. Not all the time, just when you've forgotten about it. I swear that dishwasher is possessed."

I gave Cindy a big hug. "I'm glad you're here, another person for our Gin Rummy competition!"

"Hey, I'm ready to knock Mom off her pedestal as queen of the card games." Cindy laughed.

Willa gave an all-knowing look as if to say she wasn't worried.

"So Elizabeth, tell us about your trip. How'd it go?"

"Great! We went to Santo Domingo, and we had enough time to go to a flea market. You know, with booths of stuff stacked up to the ceiling and overflowing into the walkways. We spent the whole time being chased up and down the aisles by the vendors, trying to get us to buy tacky souvenirs. They pestered the bejesus out of us. Like I would actually buy a T-shirt with the words 'Smoke More Marijuana,' emblazoned across the front! And what am I going to do with a giant three-foot-wide straw hat? Though I did find an amber bracelet."

"Amber?" Cindy perked up. "I want to see it."

"It's sooo cool, I love anything that has a mysterious mythical quality. I'm totally fascinated by the energy flow associated with amber," I said, while reaching into my bottomless tote bag to show them my find.

"Willa, you have an amber necklace. Does yours have insects in it?"

"I don't think so. I've had that necklace for ages but never checked it for insects."

"Amber is fossilized tree resin," I explained, mainly for Cindy's benefit. "The resin engulfs whatever happens to be there when it comes out of the tree. Amber jewelry can contain prehistoric insects, leaves, seeds, feathers, and all sorts of interesting objects. Can you believe it? These things are thirty million years old? Also, it glows a florescent blue color under a black light?

"Hey y'all, listen to what this pamphlet says that came with it." I started reading aloud:

"'Throughout history amber has had medicinal purposes. Its powers include love, strength, and luck. It is said to be a natural pain reliever, aid in balance, restore your energy, lower anxiety, support chakras or energy centers in the body, as well as improve joint problems such as arthritis. Amber draws power and energy to a wearer since it is electrically charged.'

"Wow." I put the pamphlet away. "I might need to buy a larger necklace for all my aches and pains. Next time you see me I'll probably look like Wilma Flintstone."

Cindy turned to Willa, with playful avarice dancing in her eyes. "You have an amber necklace? I want it."

"I don't think so," Willa said with a grin. "I've known about amber for a long time. As a matter of fact, in the early 1900s, your great uncle, Dr. Frank Chenault, used to prescribe amber to be worn around the neck for goiters and other thyroid ailments. So amber's medicinal properties were known for a long time before it showed up in *Jurassic Park.*"

"Holy cow! He lived in rural Alabama? No Internet…how did people learn about these things back then? That's amazing." Then I hesitated. "Maybe I should wear my bracelet to protect me from Jaws-the-dishwasher."

"Yeah, I need one too." Cindy looked down at her bruised shin.

Just then the phone rang. Cindy went out to the alcove off the dining room to answer it. This was back in the good old days when I first started working as a flight attendant and there wasn't anything but a landline. She came back into the kitchen.

"Elizabeth, it's for you; a real official-sounding man asking for Flight Attendant Calwell."

I ran and picked up the phone. "Hello?"

"Is this Flight Attendant Calwell?"

"Yes."

"This is John Houston with the Secret Service. You just arrived at JFK airport at 3:27 p.m. on flight 1827 from San Juan. Correct?" The serious male voice started firing questions at me.

I had to think about it for a second, I couldn't remember. "Yes. Why? What's this about?"

"You've been turned in for accepting counterfeit money on the airplane."

"What?" When I get nervous I talk fast and don't stop. "How would I know if it was counterfeit? We've never been trained to spot counterfeit anything. I wouldn't know what to look for." I continued rambling while twisting the phone cord around my finger.

"Those people drank a lot. All I did was put the liquor money in the envelope along with the other flight attendant's deposits. How… how would I know? You're sure it was me? Who is this again?"

That's when I heard my friend Peggy laughing her ass off in the background on the other end of the phone. She took the phone.

"Hey girl! We had you going there for a while."

"Peggy! You scared the 'you-know-what' out of me. I forgot your friend really works for the Secret Service. No wonder he sounded so authentic. Where are you? I thought you were on a trip."

"I'm at home. Finished my trip. Got back into Raleigh early so John and I met for a drink and decided to play a joke on you."

"Yeah, well, you two got me good. Say hey to John and tell him to watch out. I'm gunning for him now.

"Peggy, I meant to tell you to look out for my brother in the *Patch Adams* movie. It's playing on our flights this month which means I see it on every one of my trips."

"I didn't know he was an actor!"

"He lucked out as an extra so he's the one on the left side of the screen when Robin Williams does the major scene at the podium.

I always point Mike out on the monitor in the middle of the ceiling and tell all the passengers around me, 'Hey everybody, that's my brother. That's my brother, the one on the left.' The passengers love it. They all think he's a movie star. Some of 'em even clap."

"I'll be sure to watch for Mike on my next trip," Peggy said, laughing. "Tell him I'm impressed. Well, gotta run. Say hello to your Aunt Willa for me. Bye."

I returned to the kitchen. Cindy and Willa had settled in at the kitchen table with a bottle of wine.

As I grabbed a glass to join them, I said, "Remember when we came up here to visit you during the World's Fair in 1964? I passed by the Unisphere the other day. It's still right there where Mike and I as kids went to see the fair by ourselves. Can you imagine? We saw those awesome exhibits of what the future would look like with computers, and all kinds of technology that I never thought ordinary people would have.

"Mike and I rode in an amphibious car and I remember going to the Belgian Village, where we ate the biggest waffle piled high with strawberries and whipped cream. I'll never forget. I remember the two of us took the train and actually made it home…unscathed.

"I guess I know too much about what can happen, especially with my travels as a flight attendant. Hell, you have to be so cautious anywhere you go now." I cringed. "I've told you about my crewmembers who have been mugged right out in broad daylight."

"God Almighty, what is this world coming to?" Willa came out with this phrase anytime anything bad happened. "I wouldn't let any of my children do that today." She was considering how young we all were at the time. "No way."

I looked at Willa since we were reminiscing and asked, "But who lived here first, my mother or you and Uncle Buck?"

"Jean was already working in New York City at the district attorney's office when Buck was promoted and we moved here with Union Carbide."

"I don't know much about my mother's stint in New York City, except that she met my father there."

"You don't know about Murder, Inc.?" Cindy asked. "I've only heard snippets about it from Gena and Andrea one time at a family reunion."

"What's Murder, Inc.?" I looked curiously at Willa.

"Oh, it's only the most notorious Mafia trial of the century?"

"Really. That was way before my time."

"Murder, Inc. which stood for Murder, Incorporated, was the name the press gave to organized crime groups in the 1930's through the 1940's. Your mother worked in the D.A.'s office when it was all coming down." Willa leaned forward in her seat.

"Your mother was at the trial for Max 'The Jerk' Golob, one of the Mafia gangsters. He'd murdered a man, and the only eyewitness was the dead man's girlfriend. She was testifying against the mob, who had already put hits out on six hundred to a thousand souls. The D.A. was concerned about her safety, especially when it came time for her to leave the courtroom and she had to walk through the crowds of people outside."

Cindy said, "You mean the mob put a hit on her?"

"Exactly. So they put a raincoat, hat, and sunglasses on Jean, and the police escorted her right out the door through the crowd. Everyone thought your mother was the woman who had just testified. In the meantime, they snuck the prime witness out the back door of the courthouse, and she was whisked away to a safe place."

"You're talking about *my* mother? She did this? Are you sure? We're talking about the mild-mannered real estate agent from North Carolina?"

Mild-mannered—wasn't that how they referred to Superman?

"Oh yeah. She did it alright." Willa nodded her head. "Murder, Inc. was all that people were talking about at that time. There's a book and a movie about it."

"You're kidding." I just sat there stunned. "She could have been killed, and she never said a word about it." I had thought my mother had better sense than to do something like that, but then again, it was her job. Just like I never thought I would be the first line of defense against well-trained terrorists with box cutters taking over an airplane. *Wow! My mama the Super-Hero!*

"Your mother had a flamboyant life before she settled down with children." Willa yawned and stretched her arms wide, giving us the signal she was ready to turn in.

We gathered up our wine glasses, and the dishwasher door swung open right when I walked by. Jaws just missed me.

"See, I told you. It tried to get me. I'm going to have *Twilight Zone* nightmares. Stupid dishwasher." I made a point to latch it closed this time.

"Hey Cindy, if the phone rings when I'm in the shower let me know right away. I'm on reserve, and if it's crew schedule I've only got twenty minutes to call them back or else I get a missed trip on my record."

"That doesn't sound good."

"Yeah. I don't want to get fired."

Cindy and I headed up the stairs to our bedrooms.

"Night all," we said at the same time.

I hauled my luggage into my bedroom, threw my coat on the antique four-poster bed, and looked up at the two huge pictures of my grandparents in ornate wooden frames.

"Hey folks, I made it home safe from another trip."

Yes, the jetlag had finally gotten to me. I'd started talking to those long-ago dead people who stared back at me with those eyes that followed you around the room. When I was little it scared me to death. I remembered those pictures from the bedroom that I slept in in my grandparent's house. Anywhere I stood in the room, their eyes scrutinized me. One time, I even stood plastered against the wall under the picture of my grandfather; his eyeballs still stayed glued on me.

I learned years later that scientific researchers have since proved this phenomenon. Our perception of certain pictures or paintings doesn't change from different angles but this is only if the person in the portrait is facing forward. I still prefer to think of it as supernatural, similar to the tribes in Africa who don't want their photographs taken because of the fear it will steal their souls. I agree with that theory because my grandparents' souls had to have been behind those eerie eyes.

Those pictures hung in my grandparent's big antebellum house that I remembered, but Willa also filled me in about her childhood when their close-knit family lived in the original old farmhouse outside of town. My elderly aunt's stories made me appreciate how far technology has come in a relatively short period of time.

She and my mom both learned to drive one of the first cars, a Ford Model T. As a twelve-year-old, my mama sat on a pile of Sears catalogues to see over the steering wheel. They used a hand-crank wringer washing machine and sat around the radio listening to the news.

I heard many stories about my mother and her siblings, who were born shortly before World War I, and the hardship of being teenagers during the depression, following the stock market crash of 1929. Their frugal generation didn't throw out anything still useable, even penny-pinching little things, such as buttons off of old shirts. My friend, Louis, still has his grandmother's box of buttons.

Willa's habit of saving things rubbed off on me too. Just the other day, I added some more rubber bands to my stash in the kitchen drawer.

My husband asked, "Why are you saving those?"

"Willa made me do it," I said with a grin. "Besides, every time I throw something out, that's just the time when I need it."

I'm glad my job sent me to New York and gave me the opportunity to bond with Aunt Willa. She was the only one of the five siblings, of my mother's generation, still alive. Willa was a more complicated character than my mother, who had an easy-going personality that went along with raising kids in the South. Willa was a little more demanding, which coincided with living in New York. When I think about it now, Willa's three daughters would probably say just the opposite—that my mother was the more complicated character. They might be right; as a single parent, my mother had worked as a businesswoman her whole life while Willa was a stay-at-home mom.

Willa came to help my brother and me when my mother passed away from cancer. There was no such thing as hospice care back then, and since we were both still in our twenties, I don't know what we would've done without her.

As I write this, it occurs to me that is what caused Willa to quit smoking! We had all blamed my mother's awful death on her many years of smoking. Her cancer is the only thing I can imagine that could have caused Willa to quit, cold turkey, after fifty years. You've got to hand it to her; when Willa set her mind to do something she did it.

When I look back to those two years I spent with Aunt Willa, I feel grateful for having had that opportunity, and I believe everyone should contact friends and relatives whenever possible, because life is just too short. You never know what could happen, and in a split second you could lose the opportunity forever.

The generation gap between my aunt and me was similar to the gap between my niece and myself. I have tried to fill her in on what it was like when I was growing up—you know, when they had just invented fire and the wheel and there was no such thing as a computer!

No computers or cell phones, and the list goes on and on. Oh never mind…that's beyond her comprehension.

Light Bulb Moment! When did I become one of the old-fogey, geezer-generation? How could that be? I'm too young to be this old.

PLEASE TAKE 'EVERYTHING' WITH YOU

I was working with Pam, the purser, on a return flight from Santo Domingo. During the meal service, she whispered to me, "The man sitting in 6A keeps staring at me."

I backed up a step out of the galley to check out the passenger in 6A, the seat next to the window in the last row of first class. I didn't notice anything in particular about the older gentleman. He hadn't said a word to me or anyone else, insofar as I knew. So I decided to make a joke about Mr. 'No Personality.'

I told Pam, "He's not staring at me, so he must be *your* boyfriend." I clowned around with her about him, off and on, the whole flight.

"Pam, your boyfriend needs a Coke. Pam, your boyfriend wants another roll."

Our lighthearted teasing helped to pass the time, and we didn't think anything else about Mr. 6A.

Well, not until the plane landed.

I stood in the front exit area saying, "Buh-bye" to the passengers as they exited. Usually the front of the plane empties out first, but I noticed the lady in 5A standing up and frantically yelling and waving for me to come help her. From a distance, I saw her husband hadn't attempted to stand. The wife looked distraught as she pointed down in his direction.

Whispering, just loud enough for Pam to hear, I said "Aw, man! For his sake, I hope he's not having a heart attack."

Plunging into the rush of impatient passengers, I began weaving my way through like a defensive lineman on a pro football team. Eventually, I nudged my way back to the couple to see what they needed. You've heard the announcements to be careful because items may have shifted during landing. People sometimes go hunting for items, such as cell phones, that end up sliding, on the floor, to the other end of the plane.

"Sir, are you all right?"

"Look at that!" the husband and wife both shouted at the same time, while they pointed to the floor.

"Oh my! What is …?" I started laughing so hard I couldn't even finish my question.

We all looked perplexed as we tried to figure out where this set of dentures came from.

Who do you think I thought of immediately? Pam's 'boyfriend' was the only one sitting right behind this couple, so it was sort of a foregone conclusion. The rapid flow of people slowed down as the passengers paused to look, point, and burst out laughing when they passed by. By this time, the agent who'd met the flight had come back to see what all the fuss was about. We all pointed to the set of teeth. Everyone treated it like Superman's Kryptonite—no one wanted to touch this very personal, but detachable, part of the anatomy.

I yelled to Pam in the front of the plane, "Go get your boyfriend. He left his dentures on here."

Pam took off running up the jet bridge and found Mr. 6A.

She told me later that she tapped him on his shoulder and said, "Sir you left your dentures on the plane."

He gummed a reply, in a heavy Spanish accent. "*No spek Ingles.*"

Pam pointed to her teeth.

"Oh no! On *de* plane?" he asked, as he turned around to retrieve his teeth. None of us could believe he hadn't missed them. I don't know if we got any good karma for this deed, but he was very appreciative when we reunited him with his pearly whites, or maybe his *nacarado dientes blancos*.

Believe it or not, this happened to me again. I was deplaning a flight from London and walking through business class, when I spotted a bottom denture sitting on an armrest.

I yelled at the other flight attendants ahead of me, "Hey! Look what I found." Out of curiosity, I shook out the blanket on the seat and the other half of the set fell out.

The flight attendant who'd been working that side of business class held up her index finger and wagged it at all of us.

"I know exactly who these dentures belong to."

We were all astonished, "You remember the passenger?"

"Yes, I do. Mr. Mann. Mr. Drunk Mann."

❧   ❧

Here's one last denture story.

My friend Doris was working a flight in coach, looking for a bag to pick up trash. As she peered under the last row of seats, she spotted something shiny. Retrieving a flashlight to inspect the object, she discovered it was somebody's false teeth.

She called to the front of the plane to report to the purser, "You won't believe what I found back here—a set of dentures. Come help me and bring the bread tongs back with you, 'cause I can't reach them and I don't want to pick up those germy things, ugh."

This was before the airline considered it necessary to furnish us with latex gloves for picking up trash, so the purser came back with the long-handled forceps.

After they recovered the lost teeth, the purser made an announcement over the PA.

"If anyone has lost their dentures, please ring the call button."

Doris was mortified.

"If they'd been my false teeth," she said, in her Tennessee accent, "I would *not* have rung that call button for a million dollars. I'd be so embarrassed."

Doris shot a big smile with all her own teeth, way too young to have ever had any experience with partials.

But I'm sure the dentures were worth a lot more than any amount of embarrassment to the person who lost them. Think about it for a second. I have a heart attack if I find a piece of spinach in my front teeth. It's beyond my comprehension how anyone could walk around without *any* teeth.

No one responded with a call button so the purser made another attempt.

"Will everyone please look at the passengers on both sides and see if anyone is missing their teeth!"

Still no call button, even after those two unprecedented announcements, but bless her heart, the determined purser proceeded to display the teeth in a clear plastic glass and parade them up and down the aisle. As usual, most passengers had been preoccupied with reading, playing games, or sleeping and hadn't paid much attention to what was going on. Some people using sound-blocking headsets had missed the announcement altogether.

Much to the surprise of those people, she took it upon herself to hold up what looked like a science project, stopped at each row, and cross-examined each passenger herself, to see if anyone gummed a smile back at her. Still no luck.

The only false teeth I'd ever seen on display before were in our guest bedroom when I was young. They belonged to my great-aunt who used to soak them in a glass of water beside the bed at night. Early one morning, our collie, Rusty, got a hold of her dentures and then casually strolled into the kitchen with a strikingly big toothy-smile. My half-asleep mother almost dropped her cup of coffee.

My great-aunt was not nearly as upset about our dog wearing her partials, as the purser was when she went overboard in pursuit of the forgotten teeth on the airplane. It played out like a scene from the

Addams Family. In the end, nobody claimed them, and we concluded the toothless passenger must have been on a previous flight. Those false teeth could have toured the United States or even the world, for that matter, since that person had left this airplane. Maybe this could be a new category for the Guinness Book of World records: miles traveled by a pair of dentures—unaccompanied.

I think the announcement at the end of the flight needs to be changed to, "Please look around and collect all your belongings before you exit the plane...this definitely includes your teeth. Thank you for flying with us and keep smiling, *so we can see that you didn't leave them on the plane.*"

AUNT WILLA AND THE PICTURE OF A NUDE MAN

I had fun playing jokes on my Aunt Willa, and the best part of it was that she enjoyed it as much as I did.

While on a layover in Barbados, I took a picture at the beach of a really nice-looking male body-builder in a thong bathing suit. When he was lying face down on the beach towel, it appeared as if he had no clothes on at all, none whatsoever, totally *nekkid*.

I wanted to see Willa's reaction to this risqué picture so I left it on the kitchen counter next to the coffee pot. You'd better believe that picture caught my aunt's attention. She managed to hold it up close enough to her eyes to study it in detail despite her macular degeneration.

Then she exclaimed loudly, "God almighty! What has that man got on?"

"Not much," I said with a mischievous grin. "We call that kind of swimsuit 'butt floss.'"

"Butt floss?"

"Yeah, I think that's self-explanatory."

You have to understand, this was my aunt, who had once seen me in my bathing suit cover-up, a cute one-piece romper of shorts with a tank top attached at the elastic waist, and asked me, "Is that your bathing suit?"

I guess it does look like a shortened version of something she would've worn for a swimsuit back in the day.

I said, "No. Aunt Willa, you'd have a heart attack if you saw my bathing suit."

Willa was still staring at the photo.

"Your Uncle Buck and I went on vacation to Barbados, and I never saw anything like that when we were there."

She acted shocked, raised her eyebrows, and gave me the look of motherly disapproval, but the beach picture of the male centerfold somehow disappeared. Turns out she took that picture along with a whole arsenal of my stories to her weekly bridge club meeting. They had lots to talk about that week… other than recipes.

Elizabeth Calwell

WHAT AUNT WILLA AND FLYING TAUGHT
ME ABOUT LIFE

I learned a lot from living with Aunt Willa. She taught me to be thankful for everything we have. While she lived very comfortably, she didn't believe in wasting money. She never took her affluent life for granted, and I admired this quality in her.

My time with Aunt Willa also exemplified the transition between generations: past, present and future. My mother and Willa lived through the Great Depression that had a profound impact on their materialism and taught them, or rather forced them, to be frugal.

During the Depression most people were too busy worrying about where their next meal was coming from to worry about anything else. Willa told me when she was young and growing up in Russellville, Alabama, there would be a sheet of ice on the kitchen floor because the only heat for the house came from the wood-burning fireplace in the living room. The first person up had to stoke the fire and then skate across the kitchen floor to get the stove going for the day.

My friend Ruth was the youngest of nine children and the daughter of a coal miner in West Virginia. When she was young, she helped her mother make homemade soap because they couldn't afford to buy it. This process used caustic lye. Ruth accidentally dropped the lye on her foot, which melted the skin, fusing her middle three toes together. With no hospital available in the area back then, they took her to the local doctor, who managed to keep the infection from killing her.

You see I didn't have to look far for examples of why to be grateful. These stories show how lucky I am to be living today. The more I travel, the more I witness around the world, and the more I hear about the hardships others have been through, the more appreciative I am of this wonderful land we live in.

I knew my time with Aunt Willa on Long Island wouldn't be forever.

Willa would say, "You're going to miss me when I'm gone."

This was unnerving to me since I'd never heard anyone talk openly about death before. She wasn't afraid, and was ready to go because she never wanted to be the last one of her generation still alive.

I didn't know how to respond to her, so I said, "You're probably going to outlive me, considering this wacky job that I've got."

Because of macular degeneration my Aunt Willa had to move to a retirement home in South Carolina to be closer to her daughter Carolyn.

Elizabeth Calwell

After living with my aunt in the upscale residential community of Manhasset on Long Island for my first two years of flying, I now needed a new place to live and this meant a new adventure. I started looking for other accommodations close to my base in New York.

It just so happened I found a notice on the bulletin board in Ops, saying four flight attendants needed another roommate in their apartment. It was now or never. I jumped at the chance and was now off to live in midtown Manhattan, New York City.

BUH BYE! HOPE YOU HAD A GOOD FLIGHT

In my years as a flight attendant, I met a lot of interesting people from all walks of life. Some were entertaining; others have given me the gift of moments I will never forget. I will always value these experiences and the lessons I learned.

Most days are routine, but you never know when a unique experience might come out of the blue. The joy of the unexpected keeps me looking forward to every new day. It's the best part of my job. Thanks for riding along. Fly safe, and I hope you all will come back to join me again on my next flight.

APPENDIX

SUGGESTIONS FOR CHARITIES

Here are suggestions for some honest organizations. My friend Penny manages *Miracles in Action* (www.MiraclesinAction.Org) and works diligently to help indigent women in Guatemala. She takes sewing machines there from the U.S. and teaches the women a trade. All contributions to her non-profit organization will go directly to help people in need.

Also, the Airline Ambassadors is a great charity in which I participate. This is a group of volunteers, including crew members from all airlines, who offer humanitarian assistance throughout the world. Nancy Rivard, a flight attendant, is the founder, assisted by Dr. Patch Adams, of the movie fame. One of the services provided by flight attendants is to escort children and adults from foreign countries into the USA to have surgeries and medical treatments. Any and all volunteers and donations from non-airline personnel are appreciated.

ACKNOWLEDGMENTS

It really has taken a whole village to help complete this book. First of all, many thanks to Eddie Conner "Soul Intuitive" for telling me to write a book in the first place. I know he could not possibly have foreseen how much time and effort would go into this project. I read Eddie's book "Fixin' the Big BUT Syndrome," even so I still said to him, "BUT I've never written anything before." He reminded me that I tell stories all the time and I needed to share them with others. Finally he said, "Just do it," which is exactly what my Mama used to say.

I totally dismissed his ridiculous idea and left the next day on a work trip, during which three different people told me I needed to write down my stories. One even said it would make an entertaining book. I immediately looked on the internet for some kind of help which led me to the Write On group hosted by Gurpreet Jawa. Gurpreet told me I have a voice. At the time I didn't know exactly what that meant but with his continued encouragement I kept writing and rewriting and rewriting and rewriting. So here it is.

Oh, and a few months later I found out that Gurpreet in North Carolina and Eddie Conner in California were Facebook friends. They knew each other. Imagine that.

See, everything I do turns into a story.

A debt of gratitude is owed to all the flight attendants, pilots and airline personnel who contributed to my cache of tales. I work with the most amazing people.

I am also blessed to have the most amazing family and friends some of whom you met in this book.

From the Early Birds group, Noelle Granger has become an invaluable friend and go-to person. She just completed her fourth murder mystery book. I also appreciate the immense amount of help from Bob Byrd, Elizabeth Hein, Denis Dubay, Becky Abbott, Dawn Ronco and Sandy Gottlieb. My previous evening group, I would like to recognize the contributions of Diana Fritz, Jennifer Riley, Sarah Rothman, and Sean McDaniels.

From the Write On Meetup group, I need to recognize Gurpreet Jawa, Fran Applequist, Izzy Zarrillo, Sheetal Maheshwary, Kathryn Yensen, Mary Catherine Cole and the unbelievably, extraordinarily, incredibly fabulous help of Glenn Hackney who is known as the "Adverb Nazi." Sorry Glenn, I'm Southern. I can't talk without adverbs.

My various editors include: Alison Williams and Nancy R. Bailey. Also, Linda Houser who is a fabulous coach, consultant, writer, and editor. She can do anything. All three of them made me aware of issues and I learned a lot from their comments.

Renea Nelson and Lynne Peters who helped me along the way and watched it grow into a book, along with my sorority sister, Kathleen (Kathy) Morrison who read and made suggestions which only got better the more wine we drank. A shout out to all my Kappa Delta sorority sisters everywhere.

And finally I would like to thank my publisher, Drew Becker with Realization Press.

Stay tuned for my next book: "Dear Passenger: Episode II."

Also, watch for me on YouTube. I will be posting my comedy skit there soon.

Thanks y'all, this has been a lot of work but also a lot of fun.

DEFINITION of a FLIGHT ATTENDANT:

Flight at-ten-dant/

N. Actor; Acrobat; Babysitter; Baggage Handler; Ballistics Expert; Barista/Coffee Server; Bartender; Bathroom Attendant; Beverage Technician; Boss; Boxing Dummy/ Punching Bag; Busboy; Cat Herder; Chef; Circus Performer; Concierge; Confessor; Conversationalist; Counselor; Dancer; Dietitian; Dispatcher; Dreamer; Entertainer; Escape Artist; Explosives Expert; Exterminator; Firefighter; First Responder; Friend; Garbage Collector; Galley Queen; Gourmet Cook; Greeter; Gymnast; Herder; Hostess; Housekeeper; Interpreter; Janitor; Juggler; Laundress; Life Saver; Logistics Expert; Magician; Maître d'; Makeup Artist; Mechanic; Mediator; Medic; Meteorologist; Mind Reader; Miracle Worker; Mixologist; Model; Mother/Father; Motivational Speaker; MacGyver; Nanny; Negotiator; Nurse; Oracle; Order-Taker; Pen Dispenser (if I have one); Plumber; Pin Cushion; Police Officer; Porter; Pre-school Aide; Prognosticator; Psychiatrist; Psychic; Referee; Restroom Monitor; Ringmaster; Runner; Safety Inspector; Sales Person; Sanitary Engineer; Security Guard; Seer; Sky Goddess/Diva; Singer; Social Worker; Substitute Parent; Teacher; Therapist; Time-Keeper; Tour Guide; Travel Consultant/Guru; Trolley Dolly; TV Repairman; Usher; Valet; Waitress; Water Boy; Wifi Technician; Zoo Keeper. But never use the 'S' word – stewardess.

GLOSSARY

PREFLIGHT PREPARATION

AIRPLANE LINGO:

Aft - back of the plane

Airstair - the built-in stairway that opens from the rear underbelly of the fuselage and extends down to the tarmac, similar to pull-down attic stairs in a house.

Bid Line - flight crewmembers schedule for one month.

Black coffee - means coffee with nothing in it. (Alternatives are with cream, sugar or sweetener.)

Buh Bye - used to express farewell on a *Saturday Night Live* flight attendant skit.

Captain - lead pilot, four stripes on his epaulet, sits in left seat in the cockpit.

Clear Air Turbulence - unforeseen movement of air masses that can be hazardous to the comfort and safety of air travelers.

Cooper Vane - a mechanical wedge, which prevented deploying the airstair in flight. Named after D.B. Cooper who jumped out of an airplane while in flight.

Cockpit - front of plane where the pilots sit

Crew Bus - carries crew members to employee parking lot at airport

Crew schedule - airline lingo for anyone who calls from the department of coordinators to ensure proper staffing of flight crew

Deadheading - crew members being transported to another airport to go to work

Deportee - a person who has been or is being expelled from a country

Ditching - an unscheduled landing in water

F/A - flight attendant

FAA - Federal Aviation Administration

FO - First officer, the second pilot, three stripes on his epaulet, sits in the right seat

Fuselage - body of the airplane

Galley - small airplane kitchen

I.N.S. Agents - Immigration and Naturalization Service

Jump seat - folding seat designated for flight attendants

Lav - very, very small airplane bathroom

Layover - overnight rest period while on a trip

Leg - one flight segment of a trip

Mile High Club or M.H.C. - slang for the people who have had sexual intercourse while on board a flying aircraft

Operations - airport center for crew members

Pick Up - time the van will be leaving the hotel for the airport

Plucking tickets - airline terminology for checking passengers tickets at the gate (before the gate reader machines were introduced.

Purser - lead flight attendant

Senior Mamas - the most senior of flight attendants

"Slam-clickers" - what the flight attendants were called who slammed their hotel room door, and clicked the lock, never to be seen again during the entire layover.

Trip - a crew member's flight schedule that begins and ends at the crew base and may include any number of legs (flights) or days

Turn - go somewhere, turn around and come back to original departure location

TSA - Transportation Security Administration

Turbulence - the mixing of warm and cold air in the atmosphere by wind, which causes the airplane to be bumped around; classified as light, moderate, severe, or extreme.

U.M. - unaccompanied minor

Valsalva maneuver - used to equalize pressure between the ears and sinuses. Performed by pressing one's nose shut while blowing out as if blowing up a balloon.

Wicky - slang translation for whisky

Wing walkers - the ground personnel who walk under the tips of the wings during arrival and pushback of the plane.

ABOUT THE AUTHOR

Elizabeth Calwell, a graduate of East Carolina University, lives in Cary, North Carolina with her husband and her dog, along with three box turtles that live in the back yard, Trudy, Miss Piggy and Little Louis.

Having grown up in what used to be a small town gives Elizabeth a unique Southern perspective on the antics of passengers and unusual happenings while traveling.

Elizabeth still enjoys bouncing around in a metal tube at 35,000. When she is not flying she enjoys writing, painting landscapes, gardening and trips to the fabulous North Carolina beaches.

If you have any good travel stories that you would like to share please check out my web site: www.elizabethcalwell.com

If you liked this book please write a review.